Secrets
of
Heavenly
Food

by
Hajjah Naziha Adil Kabbani

INSTITUTE FOR SPIRITUAL AND CULTURAL ADVANCEMENT

© **Copyright 2009 by the Institute for Spiritual and Cultural Advancement.**
All rights reserved. Published 2009.

ISBN: 978-1-930409-71-2

No part of this book may be reproduced, stored in a retrieval system, or transmitted in any form, or by any means, electronic, mechanical, photocopying, or otherwise, without the written permission of the Islamic Supreme Council of America.

Published and Distributed by:
Institute for Spiritual and Cultural Advancement
17195 Silver Parkway, #201
Fenton, MI 48430 USA
Tel: (888) 278-6624
Fax: (810) 222-2885

Please e-mail any questions or comments to Sonia at staff@islamicsupremecouncil.org
Thank You.

Contents

Introduction by Shaykh Muhammad Nazim al-Haqqani v

Foreword by Shaykh Muhammad Hisham Kabbani vi

Author's Preface viii

About Hajjah Naziha ix

Dedication x

Acknowledgements xi

Supplications xii

Soup Chapter 1

Salad Chapter 11

Vegetable Sides Chapter 25

Egg Chapter 37

Bean Chapter 53

Bread and Pasta Chapter 63

Rice and Bulgur Chapter 83

Poultry Chapter 91

Fish Chapter 103

Stuffed Vegetable Chapter 115

Meat Chapter 129

Juice and Beverages Chapter 151

Jam and Preserve Chapter 161

Dessert Chapter 173

Index of Recipes 204

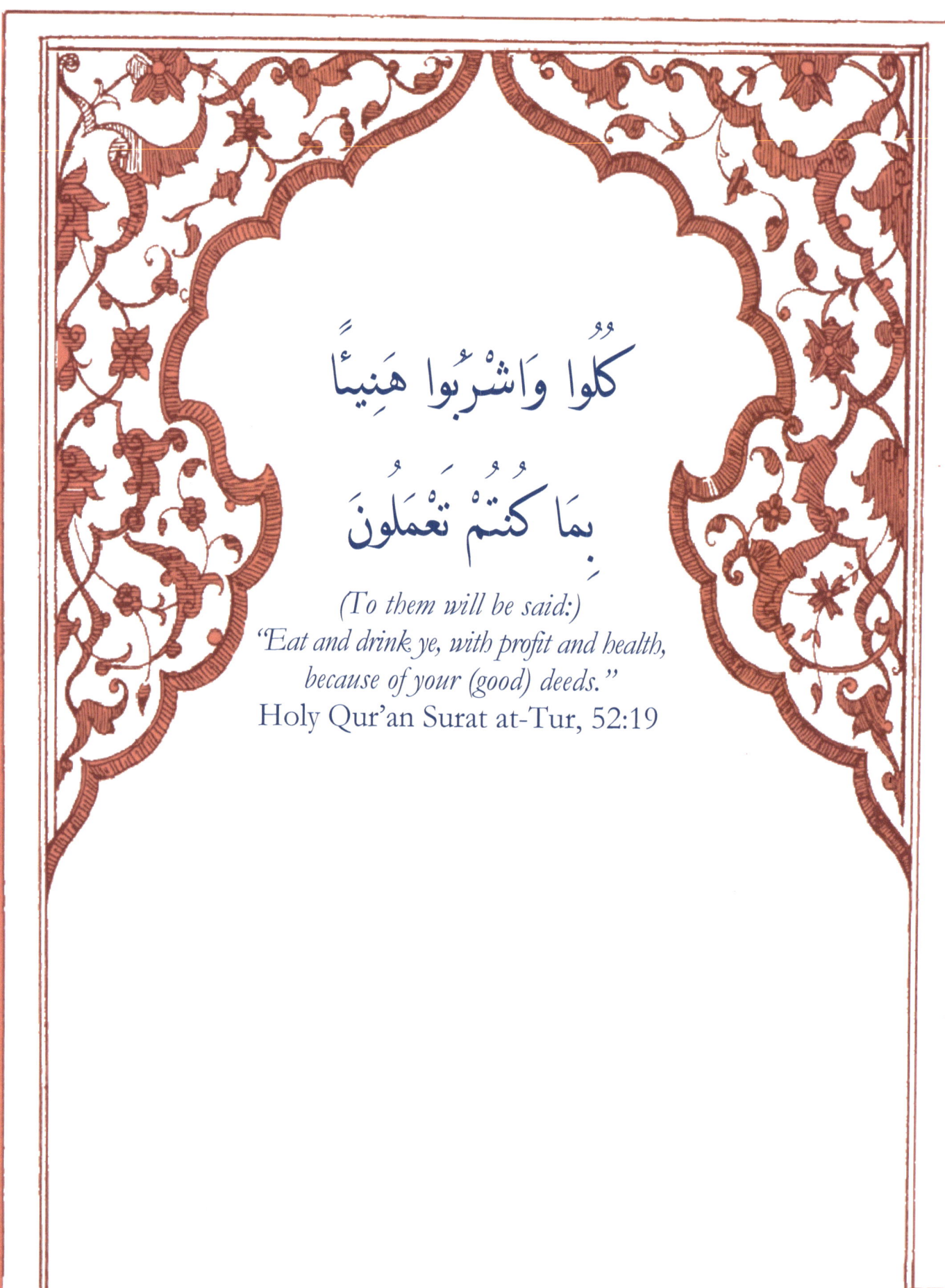

كُلُوا وَاشْرَبُوا هَنِيئًا
بِمَا كُنتُمْ تَعْمَلُونَ

(To them will be said:)
"Eat and drink ye, with profit and health,
because of your (good) deeds."
Holy Qur'an Surat at-Tur, 52:19

Introduction

by

Shaykh Muhammad Nazim Adil al-Haqqani

O my students, *mureeds* and *muhibeen*! You are like my sons and daughters, my grandchildren and great grandchildren. I have never called you to *dunya*, this worldly life, and its attractions, but only to serve your Lord humbly and with love.

Angels worship day and night without getting tired. They do not need to sleep; they are never heedless. Their food is remembrance of Allah, and praising His Beloved Sayyidina Muhammad ﷺ.

When Sayyidina Adam ﷺ ate from the tree, he, and his wife Hawwa, fell into disobedience. It was not Adam who disobeyed, but it was the seeds, the atoms, the essences of each one of his children, who moved his hand and caused him to eat. Satan had penetrated the loins of Adam and aroused in those seeds the desire to eat from the tree promising them through his tricks, that they would become angels. When they fell down on earth they were desiring to return to their home like a person who has been imprisoned or sent away from his country. That desire to be angelic was accepted by Allah.

Allah ﷻ made this earth *daar al-balaa*, the world of test and difficulties, in order to allow *dhurriyati Adam*, the descendants of Adam, to return back to their original homeland, *daar al-akhira*, in Paradise. And he provided the means to every human being to reach back to their trusts and to achieve what Allah wanted from them. Allah said, "We did not create human beings or jinn except to worship Me. I do not seek from them any provision and I do not seek any food, for verily Allah is The Provider, Owner of abundant power."

Here Allah is telling human beings, "You need Me, you need My provision and My sustenance, but I am not in need of your worship. Rather is it you who are in need of your worship and through your worship I will provide you and sustain you and feed you." Through the perfection of worship, you may reach back to that heavenly station from which you were sent down to earth; you may reach back to the position of angels – they do not need food nor drink, their sustenance is worship.

Therefore, O my sons and daughters, my grandchildren. Your real food is worship and the way to achieve perfect worship is to be sustained by holy food. Here in this book, my daughter Hajjah Naziha, has written from the many secrets of producing holy food, which is food for holiness. That is why I advised her and supported her to publish this book, because it has in it great benefits for the *mureeds*. Through these secrets and by observing carefully to be on ablution and in prayer and *dhikr* and to be conscious of Allah in every moment during preparing the food, they will find that food can power their worship much more and give them energy and purity to ascend closer and closer to our Lord's Divine Kingdom which He has promised sincere servants. I am praying that whoever opens this book with a sincere heart, seeking Allah's ﷻ good pleasure in preparing food, will find an opening to her or him and to the family which shares in the *baraka* of that food, many Divine Openings to the heart and openings of *baraka*, Divine Grace, in their daily lives.

And I am praying that such food, may be a *sabab*, a cause, for them to reach the Divine Treasures which each one has under the Divine Throne, prepared by a most Munificent and Beneficent Lord, and that they may return to the state and status of Paradise people, angelicized people, people who are ascending in Allah's Divine Mercy Oceans and blessings.

Foreword

by
Shaykh Muhammad Hisham Kabbani

A Sufi master may work to uplift his students by giving them food to eat, even food to excess. If the Shaykh dispenses more food to you—consider yourself especially fortunate, for it is food which is blessed by his hands, his prayers and his preparing it while invoking God and praising His Prophet ﷺ.

Eating for the soul means to eat only from what is pure, *halal*. Most importantly, it is food prepared with consciousness of God, His Prophet and His saints, with love, attention and intention—intention to fulfill God's Purpose in creating human beings, where He said:

I have not created jinns and men, except that they may worship Me.
(Suratu 'dh-Dhariyyah, 51:56)

Allah follows this "statement of purpose" by declaring Himself beyond the need for provision or food:

No sustenance do I require of them, nor do I require that they should feed Me.
(Suratu 'dh-Dhariyyah, 51:57)

This verse serves as a potent reminder to us of the purpose of food and its connection with *'ubudiyya*, Divine Service. Allah Alone stands in need of no one, all others besides Him are dependent on Him for nourishment and provision in every moment. Thus our attitudes towards His provision and our manners, *adab*, in preparing and consuming them are important.

The Naqshbandi shaykhs place an exceptional emphasis on the need for pure and spiritually nourishing food. Small amounts of pure food are far more valuable and provide more energy than much greater quantities of impure or contaminated food.

The Prophet ﷺ said, "the stomach is the house of illness" and his teachings concerning food, its quality, quantity and specifics of what to eat and drink form the basis for an entire branch of science known as *at-Tibb an-Nabawi*—Prophetic Medicine. It would suit us best, then, as students of such an incomparable master as Mawlana Shaykh Nazim, to observe his guidance, which in turn comes from the Sunnah of our Holy Prophet ﷺ. We should take advantage of the blessing of being able to eat from the best of what Allah has provided, thus preventing all sorts of illness from afflicting our bodies and our souls. We intend to use that sustenance for worship, and to prevent using it in following bad desires. In so doing it will be a cure for our spiritual aspects and a preparation for the afterlife.

People today do not eat to feed their soul. They are not examining the desires of the self and asking "How am I going to face God the Almighty and Exalted, on the Day of Examination, where He is going to ask us, 'Did you stop yourself from being greedy, from jealousy and from envy, from consuming what was forbidden, with your mouth and with your eyes and with your ears and with your senses? What did you benefit from the provision I sent you every day, without fail?"

Mawlana once spoke about two *mureeds* who had attained a level such that they were able to envision the Ka`bah before them when they prayed the Friday prayer. This was achieved because their wives used to prepare the food for them while in a purified state, having made ablution. When you cook having taken ablution, it gives you positive energy which then reflects to the food. Someone without ablution, such as cooks in a restaurant may cause all kinds of negative consequences to those who eat their food. That is why you find people today depressed constantly—they are filled from every side with negative energy.

In conclusion, I wish to applaud the work Hajjah Naziha has done to put together this book on holy food preparation for Sufi people and for extracting the secrets of cooking for spiritual upliftment and progress on the Path. She, and the many ladies assisting her on this project, dedicated long, arduous hours to develop the recipes, test them, document them, photograph them and then put them in book form easily usable to anyone in the kitchen.

I was fortunate to be able to "taste test" most of the recipes in this book, both over the years—for many are Hajjah's usual dishes—as well as during special events, such as 'Ashura, Eid, Mawlid and during *iftar* in holy Ramadan. Therefore I can that these recipes are delicious and have tremendous blessing.

It is my hope and prayer that not only do you enjoy the delicious dishes presented here, but you take the spiritual benefits that come in following the long line of Sufi cooks who have prepared these dishes in the past.

Shaykh Muhammad Hisham Kabbani

Author's Preface

Secrets of Heavenly Food

The first secret in cooking heavenly foods I would like to share with you is the secret of purification. It is to make ablution, *wudu*, before beginning to cook. When you cook with ablution there are countless physical and spiritual benefits. Physically, the food will be tastier to those eating it. Spiritually, when you cook with ablution, there will be powerful positive energy in the food. The energy you have in your body is transferred to the food you cook. After performing ablution you have eliminated anger from your body. Thus, the people that eat the food you cook with ablution will become peaceful and happy. Also, there are exceptional blessings in food when you cook with ablution. My mother, Hajjah Amina ق never cooked without ablution and I never cook without ablution.

On the other hand, if you cook without ablution, and with anger, the food negatively affects you and whoever else you are cooking for—your husband, your children, and your guests. The energy from this food can make those who eat it feel off-balance, nervous and worried. Thus, always cook for yourself, your family, and your guests with ablution.

Similarly, cook with feelings of love and peace. If you do, then these feelings will be transferred to the people eating. Try to be in a good mood. You are cooking for people because you love them and you want them to have good energy in their body. You are not cooking because someone is forcing you.

Also, before you start cooking, say "*Bismillahi 'r-Rahmani 'r-Raheem*" to call on Allah. While you are cooking recite *salawat* on our last Prophet, our beloved Sayyidina Muhammad.

Our food is a blessing from our Lord, Allah. For every bite of food you take to put in your mouth Allah sends over 300 angels that come and assist us to digest it. Honor the bounty that Allah blesses us with and honor the angels He sends to us by cooking with ablution and with love.

As-salaamu 'alaykum wa rahmutallahi wa barakatuhu,
Hajjah Naziha Adil Kabbani

About Hajjah Naziha

Hajjah Naziha is a descendant of the Prophet Muhammad ﷺ on both her paternal and maternal sides. She was born into a unique household, whose existence was and continues to be based purely on service to Allah. As a young child, she lived next door to Grandshaykh Abdullah Daghestani ق, master of the Naqshbandi *tariqah*. Upon his passing, her father, Mawlana Shaykh Nazim became the shaykh of the *tariqah*. Her mother Hajjah Amina Adil ق, was a scholar of Islam, who taught and wrote extensively on the lives of Allah's prophets.

Hajjah Naziha's life has not been an easy one, but it has been filled with the honor and dignity of divine service in many forms. From the time she was ten, travelers would come to stay at Grandshaykh Abdullah's home and at her father, Shaykh Nazim's home. Every day she and her mother, Hajjah Amina ق, prepared food for the shaykh and his guests, the students streaming in and out of his house without end.

They worked very hard in the household of her father, who, as the deputy of Grandshaykh was responsible for managing all the affairs of *tariqah*. They received no remuneration nor accolades, but worked sincerely, purely, to serve Allah ﷻ. When she had free time, young Naziha would run to the house of Grandshaykh Abdullah ق and attend his associations.

Before his passing, Grandshaykh Abdullah ق asked Shaykh Nazim ق for youthful Naziha's hand on behalf of Shaykh Hisham Kabbani, who was a student in the American University of Beirut at the time, in early 1969. After consulting their daughter, Shaykh Nazim ق and Hajjah Amina ق accepted the marriage.

Hajjah Naziha has traveled the world—Europe, the Middle East, the Far East, North and South America, even Alaska—with her parents and husband. And wherever she has landed, Hajjah Naziha has worked to revive the faith of the people she visits by conducting *dhikr*, speaking and bringing people back in touch with their spiritual selves. She has observed many people, cultures, and personal situations, and advises women around the world in a wide array of fields and subjects.

Hajjah Naziha has been part of the households of four saintly scholars, and through her diligence and constant association has become a scholar and advisor herself. Before his passing, Grandshaykh Abdullah ق informed Hajjah Naziha that it was Allah's decree that she be a teacher for women, and this is what has come to pass. May Allah ﷻ shower her and her family with blessings evermore, and grant them long life and good health.

The Editor

Dedication

I dedicate this book to my beloved daughter, Sajeda, and to each of my dear grandchildren. They all bring light and happiness to my life. This book, in which I have recorded part of our family's vast cultural heritage, is my legacy to them.

I also intend this for use by the women and my "daughters" in *tariqah* who will grow to be women, *Insha'Allah*. This is a guide for them to be able to cook food in the traditional Sufi way and to help them in raising their families.

I ask that you make *du'a* and pray for me as you use this book. I have given my secrets, acquired over a lifetime, on how to prepare delicious and blessed food. Many of these recipes, especially those passed down from my blessed mother, Hajjah Amina Adil ق, and from my mother-in-law Hajjah Yousra 'Alayli, may Allah bless her soul, are not available anywhere else. I ask that you read Suratu 'l-Fatihah for their blessed souls each time you use this book.

Finally, but always first and foremost, I dedicate this book to my beloved father Mawlana Shaykh Nazim Adil al-Haqqani, who taught me, love, humbleness and patience, and to my husband Shaykh Hisham Kabbani.

I hope you benefit from the *Secrets of Heavenly Food*.

Sincerely,
Hajjah Naziha Adil Kabbani

Acknowledgments

I would like to express my sincere thanks to the many people who helped with this book. Many helped in the kitchen, documenting, developing and testing recipes, and putting them in book form and with final editing and layout. I would like to specifically thank:

    Sonia Shaikh, Layla Kabbani, Hadieh Khan, Faryal Naveed,
    Salma Ammouri and Taher Siddiqui.

Supplications

Du'a before Eating

أَشْهَدُ أَنْ لَا إِلَهَ إِلَّا اللهُ وَأَشْهَدُ أَنَّ مُحَمَّداً عَبْدُهُ وَرَسُولُهُ –

أَسْتَغْفِرُ اللهَ الْعَظِيم ×3

فَإِن تَوَلَّوْا فَقُلْ حَسْبِيَ اللهُ لَا إِلَهَ إِلَّا هُوَ عَلَيْهِ تَوَكَّلْتُ وَهُوَ رَبُّ الْعَرْشِ الْعَظِيم

إِلَى شَرَفِ النَّبِي صَلَّى اللهُ عَلَيْهِ وَسَلَم وَآلِهِ وَأَصْحَابِهِ الْكِرَام، وَإِلَى أَرْوَاحِ آبَائِنَا وَأَمَّهَاتِنَا وَ حَضْرَةَ أُسْتَاذِنَا وَأُسْتَاذِ أُسْتَاذِنَا والصِّدِّيقِين الفَاتِحَة.

Ash-hadu an lā ilāha illa-Allāh wa ash-hadu anna Muḥammadan 'abduhu wa-rasūluhu, Astaghfirullāhu 'l-'Aẓīm (3x)

Fa in tawallaw faqul ḥasbīy-Allāhu lā ilāha illa Hūw. 'alayhi tawakaltu wa Hūwa rabbu 'l-'arshi 'l-'aẓīm.

Ila sharafi 'n-Nabī ṣall-Allāhu 'alayhi wa sallam, wa ālihi wa aṣḥābihi 'l-kirām wa ila arwāḥi ābā'inā wa ummuhātinā wa ḥaḍrati ustādhinā wa ustādhi ustādhinā wa 'ṣ-ṣiddīqīyyīn al-fātiḥa.

> I bear witness that there is no god but Allah and I bear witness that Muhammad is His Slave and Messenger; I ask forgiveness from Allah (3x)
> *But if they turn away, Say: "(Allah) is sufficient for me: there is no god but He: in Him I place my trust – and He is the Lord of the Throne Supreme."*
> We send this (as an offering) to the Honored Prophet ﷺ, to his family and his companions; and to the souls of our fathers, our mothers, our venerated teachers and the teachers of our teachers, and the veracious ones. (Recite) *Suratu 'l-Fatihah.*

Du'a after Eating

الحمدُ للهِ الذي أَطعمَنا وَسقَانا وَجعلنا مُسلمين، الحمدُ للهِ حمدا يُوافي نعمَهُ ويُكافي مَزيدَه كما يَنبغي لجَلال وجهكَ العَظيم يا الله، نعمةَ جَليل الله بَركةَ خَليل الله شَفاعةَ يا رَسولُ الله، اللهُمَّ أكرمْ صاحِبَ هذا الطعام والآكِلين، اللهم زد و لا تُقلّل إلى شَرفِ النَبي صلى الله عليه و سلم وآلِه وأَصحابهِ الكِرام و حَضرةَ أُستاذِنا وأُستاذِ أُستاذِنا والصِديقيين ربنا تقبل منا بحرمة سر سورة الفاتحة.

Alḥamdulillāhi 'lladhī aṭ'amanā wa saqānā wa j'alanā muslimīna. Alḥamdulillāh ḥamdan yuwāfī n'imahu wa yukāfī mazīdahu kamā yanbaghī li-jalāli wajhika 'l-'adhīm yā Allāh, n'ima jalīlullāh, barakat khalīlullāh, shafa'at yā rasūlullāh, Allāhuma 'krim ṣāḥib hadhā-ṭ-ṭ'am wa'l-ākilīn. Allāhuma zid wal ā tuqallil ila sharafi'n-Nabī ṣall-Allāhu 'alayhi wa sallam, wa ālihi wa aṣḥābihi 'l-kirām wa ila arwāḥi ābā'inā wa ummuhātinā wa ḥaḍrati ustādhinā wa ustādhi ustādhinā wa 'ṣ-ṣiddiqīyyīn. Rabbanā taqabbal minnā bi-ḥurmati sirri sūratu'l-fātiḥa.

Praise be to Allah who fed us, who quenched our thirst, and who made us to be Muslims. Praise be to Allah, a praise such that it equals to His favors, and meets His increase (of His favors); a praise which is adequate to the magnificence of your Magnificent Countenance. (Grant us) the favors of the mighty one of Allah, the blessings of the intimate friend of Allah, the intercession of the Messenger of Allah. Oh Allah honor the owner of this food and those who are eating from it. Oh Allah increase and do not diminish. We send this (as an offering) to the Honored Prophet ﷺ, to his family and his companions; and to the souls of our fathers, our mothers, our venerated teachers and the teachers of our teachers, and the veracious ones. (Recite) *Suratu 'l-Fatihah*.

Notes

Soup Chapter

Soup through the Ages

The traditional Sufi lifestyle includes partaking of soup—for important reasons. Firstly, it is considered a complete meal. When Sufi students are put into seclusion, they are served soup as meals twice a day. Secondly, soup is a special dish in the fasting month of Ramadan; it is always the first dish served after breaking the fast.

Hajjah Amina ق incorporated soup into her family's lifestyle. Hajjah Amina ق taught her children the importance of soup in cold weather, as a source of both warmth and energy, and she served soup regularly in the winter.

Many people think of soups as being full of vegetables. However, this is not always the case. Soup ingredients depend on regional availability. For instance, Hajjah Naziha's grandfather, Hajj Ali ق, who emigrated from Russia, never ate vegetable soup. Instead, he ate soups made with meat and noodles. Russia has a long winter and consequently they did not have access to a great variety of vegetables throughout the year. They only had wheat, potatoes, and corn which they could store during the long winter months. These crops were planted in the fall and harvested in spring and summer. They would dry the corn for winter. The wheat was made into flour. They had a special storage room to keep the potatoes from spoiling.

Grandshaykh Abdullah ق who was from the Daghestan area of Russia, also preferred meat and noodle soups, such as the Small Meat-Filled Dumplings in Savory Tomato Broth, Peel Meen, from his native land.

Previously, soup was only partaken in the colder, northern areas of the world. There was not a lot of variety in the soup. During the 20th century, soup gained greater prominence. It has now become famous throughout the world, not just restricted to countries with cold climates. In many elegant restaurants soup is served as the first course. Today, there exist thousands of different soup recipes around the globe.

Turkey
Kırmızı Mercimek Çorbası

Smooth Red Lentil and Carrot Soup

Ingredients
2 cups red lentils
2 medium potatoes, peeled and grated
2 carrots, peeled and grated
2 small onions, grated
2 tablespoons salt
13 cups water
3 plum tomatoes, grated (discard skin)
1 tablespoon tomato paste
1 cup milk
2 eggs
2 tablespoons flour
1 tablespoon dried mint
4 tablespoons butter, melted

Preparation
1. Wash and drain lentils. Peel and grate potatoes, carrots, and onions.
2. To a soup pot add: lentils, potatoes, carrots, onions, salt, and water. Bring to a boil on high heat, then partially uncover and boil until lentils cook around 15 to 20 minutes after it comes to a boil. Cook lentils till soft and mushy when you squeeze in between your fingers.

Note: You need potatoes and carrots to be soft; it doesn't matter if the ingredients get mushy because everything goes in the blender at the end.

3. Use a hand blender to blend all ingredients in soup pot until smooth. If using a regular blender, pour into blender and process until smooth. Return ingredients to soup pot over low heat.
4. To a separate bowl, add grated tomatoes. Stir in tomato paste. Mix well and add to soup. Bring soup to a boil again on high heat.
5. In a separate bowl, whisk milk, eggs, and flour. Mix well and add to soup. Stir in dried mint.
6. In a small saucepan, melt butter. Immediately before serving, stir into soup pot.
Serve hot.

Serves 4-6

Turkey
Pirinçli Yoğurt Çorbası

Yogurt and Rice Soup

Ingredients
½ cup short grain rice + 1 ½ cups water
2 small chicken bouillon cubes
4 pounds (64 ounces) plain yogurt
6 cups water
2 teaspoons salt
2 tablespoons cornstarch
4 egg whites
1 teaspoon dried mint
2 tablespoons butter, melted

Preparation
1. Rinse and drain rice. Place rice, 1 ½ cups water, and bouillon cubes in a small pan. Bring to a boil over high heat and cook for 10-15 minutes, or until rice is tender, and has absorbed all the water. Set aside.
2. In a separate pan, combine yogurt and 6 cups water, salt, cornstarch and egg whites. Mix well.
3. Cook over high heat. Once the yogurt starts to boil, reduce heat to low and stir in the cooked rice. Boil for 10-15 minutes on low. Add mint.
4. Drizzle melted butter on top for decoration.
5. Serve hot.

Serves 4-6

Turkey
Tavuk Çorbası

Creamy Chicken Soup

A nourishing soup, great to eat after fasting. Often eaten in the winter, to warm the body.

Ingredients

1 whole chicken with skin
2 tablespoons salt
½ teaspoon white pepper
1 medium onion whole
5 medium potatoes, peeled and cut to ½- inch cubes
1 pound carrots, peeled and cut to ½- inch cubes
8 ounces curled vermicelli noodles, crushed
12 ounces sour cream or light sour cream

Preparation

1. Place whole chicken in soup pot along with salt, pepper, whole onion, and enough water to cover by 2 inches. Bring to a boil over high heat. Reduce heat to medium-high. Boil for 45 minutes, partially covered, until chicken is tender. Skim and discard any foam produced while boiling.
2. Remove chicken to cool. Discard onion. Once chicken is cooled, debone chicken and discard skin. Tear or cut chicken into ½ -inch pieces.
3. Put potatoes and carrot cubes in chicken broth. Bring to a boil over high heat. Reduce heat to medium-high and boil for 10-15 minutes, or until potatoes are tender.
4. Add crushed vermicelli pasta. Add chicken pieces. Add sour cream to a small amount of broth, mix well, and return back to pot.
5. Cook for 5 more minutes, or until noodles are tender.
6. Serve hot.

Serves 8-10

Cyprus
Etli Pirinç Çorbası

Beef Chunk and Rice Soup

Ingredients
10 cups beef broth
1 tablespoon butter
1 small onion, finely chopped
4 plum tomatoes, grated (discard skin)
1 cup short-grain rice
1 tablespoon lemon juice
1 tablespoon parsley, chopped

Beef Broth
1 pound beef chunks, cut into 1-inch pieces
1 medium onion, roughly chopped
10-12 cups water
1 ½ teaspoons salt
½ teaspoon pepper
1 teaspoon cinnamon
2 bay leaves

Preparation
1. **Make broth:** put meat chunks, onion, and water in soup pot. Add salt, pepper, cinnamon, and bay leaves. Cover and bring to a boil over high heat. Cook for 40 minutes, or until meat is tender.
2. Remove meat from broth. Strain broth into a bowl and reserve. Discard onion and bay leaves.
3. In soup pot, melt butter and sauté onions until soft. Stir in lemon juice and grated tomatoes. Add 10 cups meat broth to pot. Add meat chunks back to soup pot. Cover and bring to a boil over high heat.
4. Rinse and drain rice. Once broth boils, add rice to pot. Stir in lemon juice.
5. Let boil for 10-15 minutes, or until rice is tender. Turn off heat. Stir in parsley.
6. Serve hot.

Serves 6-8

Turkey
Mercimekli Erişte Çorbası

Fettuccine and Lentil Soup

Ingredients
4 ½ ounces fresh, store-bought fettuccine noodles (in the refrigerated section of the grocery store. **Or** homemade noodles (1/3 **Fettuccine Noodles** recipe in **Bread and Pasta Chapter**)
2 cups brown lentils
4 teaspoons salt
1 small onion, finely chopped
½ cup olive oil, divided
¼ cup vegetable oil

Preparation
1. If using store-bought fresh fettuccine, continue to step 2. If you are making homemade fettuccine, use fettuccine recipe from Bread and Pasta chapter.
2. Wash lentils. Soak lentils for 30 minutes. Drain lentils.
3. To a soup pot add: lentils, 8 cups of water, and salt. Cover pot. Bring to a boil over high heat. Reduce heat to medium and continue boiling for 15-20 minutes, or until lentils are softened, but still firm. Mix in ¼ cup of the olive oil.
4. Cut fettuccine into 2-inch pieces. Add fettuccine pieces.
5. In a saucepan, heat vegetable oil and remaining ¼ cup of olive oil on high heat. When hot, add the onion and sauté until dark golden. Stir onions and any pan drippings into soup pot.
6. Cook partially covered, over low heat for 5-15 minutes, or until fettuccine is tender.

Note: Homemade fettuccine takes longer to cook.

7. Serve hot.

Serves 4-6

Syria
Haraaq Usba'

Pomegranate-Flavored Fettuccine and Lentil Soup

A highly flavorful soup!

Ingredients
4 ½ ounces fresh, store-bought fettuccine noodles (in the refrigerated section of the grocery store. **Or** homemade noodles (1/3 **Fettuccine Noodles** recipe in **Bread and Pasta Chapter**)
2 cups brown lentils
1 small onion, finely chopped
½ cup olive oil, divided
¼ cup corn oil
4 teaspoons salt
¾ cup pomegranate juice or 1-2 tablespoons pomegranate molasses
2 teaspoons dry basil

Preparation
1. If using store-bought fresh fettuccine, continue to step 2. If you are making homemade fettuccine, use fettuccine recipe from Bread and Pasta chapter.
2. Wash lentils. Soak the lentils for 30 minutes. Drain lentils.
3. **To a soup pot add:** lentils, 8 cups of water, and salt. Cover pot. Bring to a boil over high heat. Reduce heat to medium and continue boiling for 15-20 minutes, or until lentils are softened, but still firm. Mix in ¼ cup of the olive oil.
4. Cut fettuccine into 2-inch pieces. Add fettuccine pieces.
5. In a saucepan, heat corn oil and remaining ¼ cup of olive oil on high heat. When hot, add chopped onions and sauté until dark golden. Stir onions and any pan drippings into soup pot.
6. Cook partially covered, over low heat for 5-15 minutes, or until fettuccine is tender. Stir in pomegranate juice and basil. Let simmer for 5 minutes.
7. Serve hot.

Serves 4-6

Turkey
Domates Çorbası

Creamy Tomato Soup

Ingredients
5 cups tomato juice (from 8 large tomatoes)
½ cup water
2 bay leaves
4 small chicken bullion cubes
1 ½ onions, finely chopped
3 teaspoons dried basil
1 ¾ teaspoons salt
½ to ¾ teaspoon pepper (adjust to taste)
1/8 cup flour
1/8 cup butter
9 ounces evaporated milk

Preparation
1. If using fresh tomatoes, quarter and blend until juiced. Once blended, put juice through a food mill or pour through a large metal strainer to strain tomato seeds. Discard seeds.
2. **To a soup pot add:** tomato juice, bay leaf, bouillon cubes, onions, dried basil, salt, and pepper. Bring to a boil over high heat. Reduce heat to medium high and cover. Continue boiling for 15 minutes, stirring occasionally.
3. In a separate saucepan, heat butter over medium heat. When melted, gradually add flour, stirring constantly with a wooden spoon.
When thoroughly mixed and a golden color, stir in evaporated milk. Mix well. Stir in 1 cup of the tomato juice from soup pot.
4. Add flour-tomato mixture to soup pot. Simmer over medium heat. Discard bay leaves. Using a hand blender, blend until smooth.
5. Serve hot.

Serves 5-7

Turkey
Havuç Çorbası

Carrot Soup

Ingredients
4 tablespoons butter
2 pounds carrots, peeled and cut into ½-inch cubes
2 medium potatoes, peeled and cut into ½-inch cubes
6 small beef bouillon cubes
9 cups water
1 ½ teaspoons salt
¼ teaspoon white pepper
½ teaspoon sugar
1 large onion, finely chopped
½ cup chopped parsley for decoration

Preparation
1. Melt butter over medium-high heat in a soup pot. Sauté carrots and potatoes for 10-15 minutes, or until carrots are soft.
2. Pour water into the soup pot. Dissolve beef bouillon cubes in water.
3. Stir chopped onions into the broth.
4. Stir in salt, pepper, and sugar.
5. Bring to a boil over high heat. Boil uncovered for 3 minutes, or until potatoes are tender. Once the vegetables are cooked; blend using a hand blender or ladle the soup into a blender in batches. Blend until smooth and transfer to a serving tureen.
6. Pour into a soup tureen and decorate with parsley.
7. Serve hot.

Serves 6-8

Cyprus
Pırasa Çorbası

Leek Soup

Ingredients
6 leek bulbs (the white part of the leeks)
6 tablespoons butter
8 cups water
6 small chicken bouillon cubes
6 tablespoons flour
1 cup milk
1 teaspoon salt
½ teaspoon white pepper
2 tablespoons sour cream

Preparation
1. Remove bulbs from green leek stems. Cut bulbs in half lengthwise. Make ¼ inch slices. Wash well. Put in a bowl with cold water, and separate the cut leeks. Let sit in water to get the dirt out. Rinse thoroughly and drain.
2. Heat 2 tablespoons of butter in a soup pot. When melted, sauté the leeks for 2-5 minutes, or until soft. Add water and bouillon cubes to the leeks. Bring to a boil over high heat. Blend soup in pot with hand blender.
3. In a separate bowl, whisk together flour, milk, salt, pepper, and sour cream. Stir into soup pot. Boil together with leeks for 5 minutes.
4. In a small saucepan, melt remaining four tablespoons of butter. Pour on top of the soup when ready to serve.
5. Serve hot.

Serves 6-8

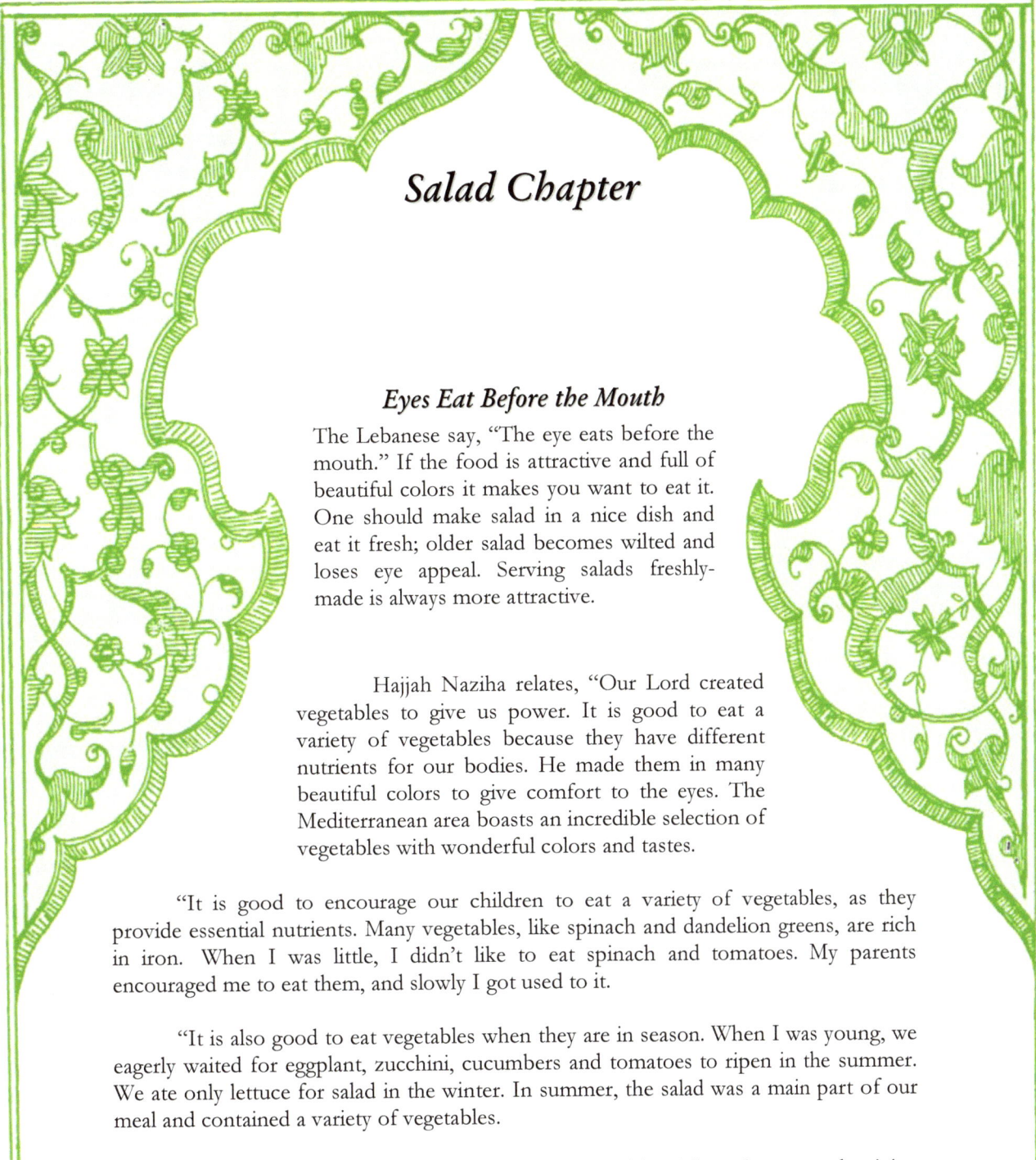

Salad Chapter

Eyes Eat Before the Mouth

The Lebanese say, "The eye eats before the mouth." If the food is attractive and full of beautiful colors it makes you want to eat it. One should make salad in a nice dish and eat it fresh; older salad becomes wilted and loses eye appeal. Serving salads freshly-made is always more attractive.

Hajjah Naziha relates, "Our Lord created vegetables to give us power. It is good to eat a variety of vegetables because they have different nutrients for our bodies. He made them in many beautiful colors to give comfort to the eyes. The Mediterranean area boasts an incredible selection of vegetables with wonderful colors and tastes.

"It is good to encourage our children to eat a variety of vegetables, as they provide essential nutrients. Many vegetables, like spinach and dandelion greens, are rich in iron. When I was little, I didn't like to eat spinach and tomatoes. My parents encouraged me to eat them, and slowly I got used to it.

"It is also good to eat vegetables when they are in season. When I was young, we eagerly waited for eggplant, zucchini, cucumbers and tomatoes to ripen in the summer. We ate only lettuce for salad in the winter. In summer, the salad was a main part of our meal and contained a variety of vegetables.

"In the beginning, people ate only raw vegetables. Then they started mixing different vegetables with each other, and this is how the first simple salad appeared. Then they found they could cook certain kinds of vegetables but that some, like cucumbers, are better raw."

Green Fava Bean Preparation

Preparation

1. Prepare fresh fava beans: Cut off both ends of the fava pods (which look like large pea pods).

2. ▲Using a knife, remove string from all around the pods.

3. ▲Discard string.

3. ▲Cut fava bean pods into 3/4-inch pieces.

4. ▲Rinse beans.

5. ▲Place cut fava bean pods and beans directly into a bowl. Fill with water. Cut a lemon in half and squeeze juice into bowl to prevent blackening. Then cut lemon into more pieces and add to bowl.
6. When ready to use, drain fava beans and discard lemon.

Cyprus
Sirrkali Pakla Salatasi

Fresh Fava Beans and Garlic

Ingredients
2 pounds fresh fava beans
1/3 cup + 2 tablespoons olive oil
¼ cup vinegar, preferably balsamic
2 teaspoons crushed garlic cloves
1 ½ teaspoons salt, divided

Preparation
1. Follow directions in **Green Fava Bean Preparation on page 122**.

2. ▲**To a pot add:** beans and water to cover. Mix in 1 teaspoon salt.

3. Cover pot and bring to a boil on high heat. Reduce heat to medium and cook 15 minutes. Strain beans. Pour into a serving bowl.
4. Prepare dressing. To a small bowl add: olive oil, vinegar, garlic, and salt.
5. Pour dressing over cooked fava beans. Mix well.
6. Serve at room temperature or refrigerate and serve cold.

Serves 4-6

Cyprus
Kolandro Salatası

Green Olive and Cilantro Salad

Ingredients
2 bunches minced cilantro
¼ cup green olives (unpitted)
¼ cup lemon juice
¼ cup olive oil
¼ teaspoon salt

Preparation
1. Mix cilantro and olives in a small bowl.
2. Add lemon juice, olive oil, and salt. Mix well.
3. Serve at room temperature.

Serves 4

Cyprus
Pancar Salatası

Beet Salad

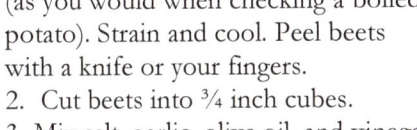

Ingredients
11 fresh beets
2 cloves finely chopped garlic
1 teaspoon salt
¼ cup olive oil
¼ cup balsamic vinegar

Preparation
1. Place beets in a pot with enough water to cover by 2 inches. Bring to a boil over high heat and continue to boil for 15-20 minutes, or until an inserted fork pulls out with ease (as you would when checking a boiled potato). Strain and cool. Peel beets with a knife or your fingers.
2. Cut beets into ¾ inch cubes.
3. Mix salt, garlic, olive oil, and vinegar in a small bowl. Pour over beets and mix well. Refrigerate.
4. Serve cold.

Serves 4-6

Cyprus
Lahana Salatası

Cabbage Salad

Ingredients

1 pound shredded white cabbage
¾ cup orange juice
1 teaspoon salt
¼ cup olive oil

Preparation

1. Remove and discard outer cabbage leaves. Cabbage does not need to be washed.

2. ▲ Slice off a chunk of cabbage next to core.

3. ▲ Then thinly slice cabbage at an angle. Change the direction of the slices to make cabbage pieces smaller. As you cut, remove and discard any hard stems from cabbage leaves.
4. Put cabbage in a medium-sized serving bowl. Mix orange juice, salt, and olive oil in a small bowl. Pour over cabbage. Toss cabbage and dressing.
5. Serve at room temperature.

Serves 6-8

Cyprus
Havuçlu Turp Salatası

Carrot and Radish Salad

Ingredients
3 large grated carrots
10 grated radishes
¼ cup lemon juice
¼ cup olive oil
1 teaspoon salt

Preparation
1. Combine grated carrots and radish heads in a medium-sized serving bowl.
2. Mix lemon juice, olive oil, and salt in a small bowl. Pour over carrots and radishes. Toss vegetables and dressing.
3. Serve at room temperature.

Serves 2-4

Middle East
Patlıcan Salatası

Eggplant Salad

Ingredients
4 medium eggplants
1 teaspoon salt
½ cup lemon juice
1¼ cup olive oil
4 tablespoons finely chopped parsley
1 finely chopped green onion
    (optional)

Garnish
1 chopped plum tomato
2 tablespoons finely chopped parsley

Preparation
1. Cook whole eggplants under high heat broiler for approximately 20 minutes, or until soft. Carefully turn eggplants while broiling to ensure even cooking. If you don't turn them, the top part of the eggplants (by the broiler) will burn.
2. Once eggplants are cooked, submerge in cold water. Cut off stem. Remove skin either by peeling off with your fingers or cutting with a small knife.
3. Cut eggplant into small pieces and place in a mixing bowl.
4. Mix salt, lemon juice, and olive oil into eggplant.
5. Add parsley and onions to eggplant. Mix well. Transfer to a shallow serving bowl.
6. Garnish eggplant with combined tomato and parsley.
7. Serve at room temperature.

Serves 4

Cyprus
Kuru Bakla Salatası

Fava Bean Salad

Ingredients

6 cups dry flat, wide fava beans
    (available at Middle Eastern stores)
1 tablespoon baking soda
1 whole head garlic
¾ cup olive oil
¾ cup lemon juice or balsamic
    vinegar
1 teaspoon salt
3 ½ tablespoons chopped parsley
2 tablespoons olive oil

▲Wide fava beans

Preparation

1. ▲Soak fava beans overnight in hot water (enough to cover) and baking soda.

2. ▲In the morning, drain the fava beans and peel brown skin from them. To peel, start by cutting black side with a small knife. Then the outer skin will come off easily.

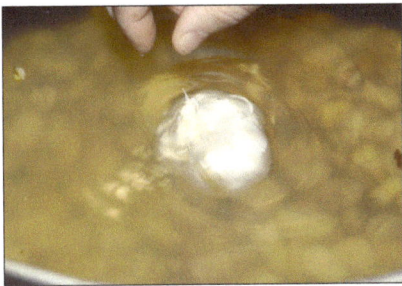

3. ▲Boil beans in a soup pot with fresh water to cover the beans by about three inches and whole garlic head. Boil on high heat for 45 minutes.
4. Drain beans. Place in a bowl. Reserve boiled head of garlic.
5. Mix olive oil, lemon juice (or balsamic vinegar), and salt in a small bowl. Pour over beans. Sprinkle parsley over top. Place boiled head of garlic in center for decoration.
6. Drizzle with olive oil..
7. Serve at room temperature.

Serves 4-6

Cyprus
Yumurtalı Patates Salatası

Parsley-Flavored Potato and Egg Salad

Ingredients
5 medium potatoes
5 eggs
2 tablespoons minced parsley

Dressing
¼ cup lemon juice
¼ cup olive oil
½ teaspoon salt
¼ teaspoon pepper

Preparation
1. Place potatoes in a pot with enough cold water to cover. Cover and cook on high heat. When the water boils, uncover and boil potatoes for 15 minutes, or until cooked. To test if potatoes are cooked, insert a fork into the potatoes. If it comes out easily, then the potatoes are cooked. If not, then continue boiling until cooked.
2. Place eggs in a separate pot with enough cold water to cover.
3. Add some salt to the water. Boil eggs in pot until cooked.

Note: Cooking the eggs with a little bit of salt helps them to peel easily when they're cooked. Also, there is an interesting way to check if the eggs are cooked. Try to spin the egg. If the egg spins evenly and stays in one spot then it is cooked. If the egg wobbles then it needs to cook longer.

4. Peel potatoes and eggs. Cut potatoes into 1-inch pieces. Cut eggs into small chunks. Combine the potatoes and eggs in a large bowl.
5. Prepare the dressing: mix the lemon juice, olive oil, salt, and pepper, in a small bowl.
6. Mix parsley into the potatoes and eggs. Add dressing and mix well.
7. Serve at room temperature.

Serves 2-4

Middle East
Kırmızı Biber Salatası

Roasted Bell Pepper Salad

Hajjah Naziha's adaptation of a roasted bell pepper salad.

Ingredients

4 bell peppers, (assorted colors)
¼ cup olive oil
½ cup lemon juice
1/3 cup minced cilantro
1 clove finely chopped garlic
4 teaspoons salt

Preparation

1. Cook whole peppers under a high heat broiler for approximately 20 minutes, or until soft. Carefully turn peppers while broiling to ensure even cooking.
2. Submerge cooked peppers in cold water. Remove skin with a small knife. Cut peppers into small, 1-inch pieces. Place in a mixing bowl.
3. Add olive oil, lemon juice, cilantro, garlic, and salt to peppers. Mix well.
4. Serve at room temperature.

Serves 4

Turkey
Çoban Salatası

Tomato and Cucumber Salad

Ingredients

1 pound cubed cucumbers (about 3 cucumbers)
2 chopped plum tomatoes
1 finely chopped small onion
¼ cup lemon juice or balsamic vinegar
¼ cup olive oil
¼ teaspoon salt

Preparation

1. Mix cucumbers, tomatoes, onions, lemon juice (or balsamic vinegar), olive oil, and salt in a bowl.
2. Serve at room temperature.

Serves 2-4

Lebanon
Treedah

Zucchini Salad

A good dish to prepare alongside the stuffed Zucchini and Yogurt dish in the **Stuffed Vegetables Chapter;** the insides of the zucchini are made into their own delicious salad.

Ingredients
3 cups peeled and grated zucchini
1 finely chopped small onion
1 finely chopped clove garlic
1 teaspoon plus 2 tablespoons olive oil
2 tablespoons lemon juice, preferably fresh
¼ teaspoon salt
2 tablespoons dried mint

Preparation
1. Put zucchini and onions in saucepan with enough water to cover. Bring to a boil over high heat. Reduce heat to medium-high and cook, uncovered, for 10 minutes.
2. Pour zucchini into a metal strainer and place strainer over the saucepan to drain. Press gently on the zucchini with the back of a spoon to squeeze out excess water.
3. Let drain for 5-10 minutes.
4. Put zucchini and onion in a serving bowl. Add garlic, olive oil, lemon juice, salt, and mint. Mix well.
Serve at room temperature.

Serves 2-4

Notes

Vegetable Sides Chapter

Mediterranean Vegetable Dishes

Mediterranean people love vegetable dishes, especially in the summer when the weather is very hot and lots of seasonal vegetables grow. They consume very little meat, and family kitchens are full of a variety of cooked vegetables.

Hajjah Naziha narrates, "When we lived in Damascus my father [Shaykh Nazim] would often say 'I don't want to eat any heavy food today. Just fry eggplant and sprinkle it with crushed garlic. We can eat that with bread and salad.' Out of respect for my father, my mother would give him his own plate. Then she would share a plate with me and my brothers and sister. That was a typical summertime dinner for our family.

"We often grew our own vegetables in the summer. One year my uncle built a wooden trellis in our garden for grape vines to grow on. The vines grew so thick and tall that they would make shade in the garden. He planted the grape vines in the beginning of fall, and they bloomed the following summer, and they continue to bloom every summer. There were leaves of many different sizes; some would become very large. My mother told me to pick the soft, smaller leaves from the tips of the branches. These leaves are more tender than the larger ones, and they cook more quickly.

"We would sit together and prepare the filling with the ingredients from our garden and pantry. I would chop tomatoes and onions. My mother would mix the cut vegetables with rice, olive oil, and seasoning to make a filling. Then we would sit together, and she showed me the correct place to put the stuffing on the leaves. We rolled them together. Then she would cook the rolled leaves, and that would be our family's lunch or dinner for the day. We continue to eat vegetable dishes in the summer; both because they are plentiful and they make a light summer meal."

Lebanon
Bataata bil-Kizbara

Cilantro and Garlic Flavored Potatoes

Ingredients
1 cup vegetable oil (for frying)
1 ½ teaspoons salt, divided
5 medium potatoes, peeled and cut into 1 ½-inch cubes
1/3 cup vegetable oil
1½ tablespoons chopped garlic
¾ cup chopped cilantro
¼ cup lemon juice

Preparation
1. Heat oil over high heat. Add ½ teaspoon of salt to avoid splattering. Fry potatoes in batches until golden brown. Remove from oil with a slotted spoon.
2. In a separate large pan, heat 1/3 cup of oil on high heat. Add garlic and sauté until golden. Add cilantro. Cook together for 2-3 minutes. Mix in remaining salt and lemon juice. Add cooked potatoes and cook together for 5 minutes, stirring occasionally.
3. Serve warm, with pita bread and lemon.

Serves 2-4

Turkey
Kimyonlu Patates

Cumin-Spiced Potatoes

Ingredients
5 large potatoes
4 tablespoons vegetable oil
4 tablespoons olive oil
1 large onion, finely chopped
1 teaspoon salt
½ teaspoon pepper
1 teaspoon cumin
1 teaspoon paprika or ½ teaspoon chili pepper

Preparation
1. Place potatoes in a pot with water to cover. Bring to a boil over high heat. Boil uncovered for 20 minutes, or until potatoes become tender.
2. Drain and peel potatoes. Cut into 1-inch cubes.

3. ▲ Heat both oils in a frying pan on high heat. Add onion and fry until golden brown.
4. Add potatoes, salt, pepper, cumin, and paprika (or chili) to onions. Reduce heat to medium. Cook together for 5-10 minutes, stirring occasionally.
5. Place into a serving bowl.
6. Serve warm.

Serves 2-4

Cyprus
Zeytinyağlı Kabak

Zucchini with Onions and Tomatoes

Ingredients
¼ cup vegetable oil
¼ cup olive oil
1 large chopped onion
4 chopped plum tomatoes
4 pounds Arab zucchini, cut into ½-moon shapes
1 head garlic, broken into cloves and peeled
1 ½ tablespoons salt
1 teaspoon pepper
¼ cup lemon juice
2 teaspoons dried mint

Preparation
1. Heat both oils in a pot on high heat. Add onions and fry until they are just about to brown. Add tomatoes. Cover and cook about 5 minutes, until tomatoes release their juices.

2. ▲ Add zucchini, garlic cloves, salt, and pepper. Bring to a boil on high heat, covered. Reduce heat to medium and cook, partially covered, for 25 minutes, or until zucchini is tender. Add lemon juice and cook together for 5 more minutes.

Note: Don't stir zucchini too much or it will break.
3. Transfer to a serving dish. Sprinkle with dry mint.
4. Serve at room temperature.

Serves 4-6

Cyprus
Karnıbahar Salatası

Tangy Cauliflower Florets

Ingredients
1 small cauliflower head, or 1 ¼ pounds cauliflower florets
¼ cup olive oil
¼ cup lemon juice
½-1 teaspoon salt (to taste)
½ teaspoon crushed garlic (optional)

Garnish
Leaves from a sprig of parsley

Preparation
1. If using florets, go to step 2. If using a whole cauliflower, cut into florets.
2. Put cauliflower florets into a pot of cold water. Bring to a boil over high heat. Boil, uncovered, for 15 minutes, or until tender.
3. Drain cauliflower and add to a large bowl along with olive oil, lemon juice, salt, and garlic. Mix well so cauliflower absorbs the seasoning flavors.
4. Garnish with parsley.
5. Serve at room temperature or refrigerate and serve cold.

Serves 4-6

Lebanon
Salaatat A`wad as-Silaq bil-Laban

Chard Stems with Yogurt

Ingredients

1 ½ cups chopped chard stems
1 cup plain yogurt
2 cloves chopped garlic
½ teaspoon salt
2 teaspoons olive oil (drizzle on top)
¼ cup Tahini (optional)

Preparation

1. ▲ Cut chard stems.
Note: Use leaves for the **Chard and Black Eyed Peas** in this chapter or the **Stuffed Swiss Chard** in the **Stuffed Vegetables Chapter**.

2. Place stems in pot and bring to a boil over high heat. Boil uncovered for 10 minutes, or until stems become tender. Drain. Place stems in a bowl.
3. In a separate bowl mix yogurt, garlic, and salt. Pour yogurt mixture over chard. Mix well.
Optional: You may add ¼ cup Tahini to this dish for a tasty variation.
4. Transfer to a serving dish and drizzle with olive oil.
5. Serve chilled.

Serves 2

Lebanon
Hindiba biz-Zayt

Dandelion Greens

Ingredients
3 pounds (about 8 bunches) dandelion greens
¾ cup olive oil
3 large onions, thinly sliced
4 garlic cloves, cut into thin circles
1 teaspoon salt
1 teaspoon cinnamon
4 ½ tablespoons lemon juice

Garnish
1-2 tablespoons olive oil

Preparation
1. Cut the roots off of the dandelions and discard.

2. ▲ Separate the leaves.

3. ▲ Chop leaves into 1-inch pieces. Place in a strainer and rinse.
4. In a soup pot, place the dandelion leaves and cover with water. Bring to a boil on high heat. Boil the greens for 30 minutes. Drain and rinse with cold water. Leave in a strainer. Squeeze out water from dandelions with your hands. Set aside.
5. Heat olive oil in a frying pan on high heat. When hot, add the onions and cook until a dark golden brown. Remove the onions from the oil with a slotted spoon and set aside.

6. ▲ Cook garlic circles in same oil for one minute, or until golden brown.
7. Add the dandelion leaves to the garlic. Reduce heat to medium-low. Add salt and cinnamon and cook for 10 minutes. Add lemon juice and cook for another ten minutes.
8. Transfer to a serving plate. Sprinkle reserved browned onions over the top.
9. Drizzle with 1-2 tablespoons of olive oil.
10. Serve at room temperature.

Serves 4-6

Mediterranean
Waraq `Anab biz-Zayt

Vegetarian Grape Leaves

Stuffed grape leaves are a popular dish all over the Mediterranean region. There are notable regional differences in the preparation of grape leaves. Cypriots often use dried mint as a seasoning whereas Lebanese use parsley. Turks cook the stuffing a bit before rolling the grape leaves.

Ingredients

1 pound (1 16-ounce jar) grape leaves or fresh grapes leaves
3 cups short-grain rice
6 large tomatoes, diced
1 ½ bunches minced parsley
2 tablespoons salt
1 ½ cups lemon juice
1 ½ cups olive oil
3 small onions, finely chopped
1 large potato, peeled and sliced into ¼-inch rounds

Sauce Ingredients

1 ½ cups water
½ cup lemon juice
¼ cup olive oil

Preparation

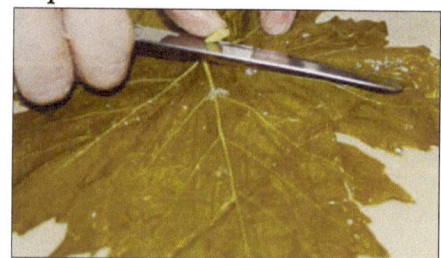

1. ▲ Cut the stems off of the leaves.
2. If using leaves from a jar, rinse and drain the leaves with cold water. Soak drained grape leaves in a bowl of hot water to soften them. Go to Step 4.
3. If using fresh leaves, boil in water for approximately 5 minutes, or until the leaves are tender and slightly yellow in color. Drain and rinse under cold water.
4. Prepare stuffing: mix rice, tomato, parsley, salt, lemon juice and olive oil in a bowl.

Prepare leaves: the leaves have 2 different sides. One side is heavily veined, and one side is smooth and "shiny." Take a leaf and put the smooth, shiny-side down on the counter.

5. ▲ Place one tablespoon of rice mixture at the bottom of the leaf, at stem's edge.

6. ▲ Fold in the sides of the leaf so they cover the rice and then begin rolling, tightly but carefully to avoid breaking the leaf. Continue until all the filling is used up.

7. ▲ Roll the dolmas so they are about 2 inches long and ½-inch wide.

8. ▲ Place potato slices in a 5-quart pot to cover the bottom; this will prevent grape leaves from sticking when they cook. Place rolled dolmas in pot on top of potatoes so that the "seam" is on the bottom.
9. Place grape leaves in tightly-packed rows.
10. Prepare sauce: mix water, lemon juice and olive oil. Set aside.+.+

11. ▲ Before pouring sauce into pot, put a dinner plate that is slightly smaller than the circumference of the pot on top of the dolmas. Secure by placing a bowl full of water on top. This way the grape leaves don't open and float when you add the sauce.
12. Pour sauce in from the side of the pot, between the plate and the pot. Keep adding the water until the sauce reaches to two inches above the plate.
13. Cook over high heat until the sauce comes to a boil. Reduce heat to medium and simmer for 15 minutes. Remove bowl of water, but keep the plate on. Reduce heat to low and cook for an additional 35-45 minutes, or until done.

Note: Test to see that the dolmas are done by tasting one (let cool first). If the rice is soft and the leaves are tender, they're done. If the rice is still hard and the sauce has decreased, add enough water to reach ¾-inch above the plate and continue to cook. After cooking, there will be a little bit of sauce left.

14. ▲ Once cooked, remove the pot to a sink full of icy cold water.
15. Remove dolmas, one at a time, and place onto a serving plate. Arrange potatoes around the edge or on top. The potatoes have a lovely flavor, having absorbed the flavor of the grape leaves and sauce.
16. Serve at room temperature or cold with salad.

Serves 6-8

Turkey
Zeytinyağlı Biber Dolması

Vegetarian Stuffed Bell Peppers

Ingredients
8-10 small bell peppers, assorted colors
1 medium tomato, sliced into rounds

Filling
1 cup short grain rice
2 teaspoons salt, divided
¼ cup olive oil
2 tablespoons pine nuts
1 medium onion, chopped
2 tablespoons raisins
1 tablespoon tomato paste
1 teaspoon sugar
2 teaspoons dry mint
½ teaspoon cinnamon
1 teaspoon chili pepper (optional)
1½ cups water

Sauce
5 cups water
1 teaspoon salt

Preparation
1. Rinse rice and soak in hot water and 1 teaspoon of the salt for 30 minutes.
2. Prepare filling: warm olive oil over medium-high heat in a frying pan. When hot, add pine nuts and sauté until golden brown. Add onions to pine nuts and sauté until onions are soft. Mix in raisins and tomato paste. Sauté together for 2 minutes.
3. Add 1 teaspoon of the salt, sugar, mint, cinnamon, and chili (optional) to pan. Mix well. Stir in soaked rice. Add 1½ cups water. Cook, covered, on low heat for 20 minutes, or until rice is tender. Remove from heat and transfer to a plate to cool.
Note: You can also use this filling for stuffed grape leaves or cabbage.

4. ▲ Core peppers: cut around stem of peppers and remove seeds. Rinse peppers and leave upside down to drain excess water.

5. ▲ Stuff peppers with 6-8 tablespoons of filling (depending on size of pepper).
Note: Avoid packing down the stuffing, as this will not allow the rice to cook properly.

6. ▲ Place stuffed peppers into a 6 quart pot. Place a tomato slice on the top of each stuffed pepper as a lid. This adds flavor and prevents rice from overflowing.
7. Mix 1 teaspoon salt into 5 cups water. Pour into pot. The sauce should cover about three quarters of the peppers. Bring to a boil over high heat. Reduce heat to low and cook, uncovered, for 30 minutes.
8. Serve at room temperature or refrigerate and serve cold. Often eaten cold in the summer.

Serves 4-6

Lebanon
Loubeeya musallat ma` Silaq

Chard and Black-Eyed Peas

Ingredients
1 cup dry black-eyed peas
5 cups cut chard, about 1 bunch or 5 stems of chard
¼ cup vegetable oil
¼ cup olive oil
5 cloves chopped garlic
1 bunch chopped cilantro
1 teaspoon salt
½ cup lemon juice

Garnish
¼ cup vegetable oil
1 ½ onions, thinly sliced

Preparation
1. Soak black-eyed peas overnight in hot water. Drain. Place peas in a pot with water to cover. Bring to a boil over high heat. Boil uncovered for 20 minutes, or until peas become tender. Drain and set aside.

2. ▲Prepare chard leaves: cut off stem. Cut out stem that goes into the leaf. Slice chard leaves into ½ inch-wide strips. Cut strips lengthwise to make each piece about 1 ½ inches long.
3. Heat vegetable and olive oils in a soup pot. Add garlic and cilantro. Sauté for 2 minutes. Add chard and sauté for 5 more minutes.
4. Stir black-eyed peas into chard mixture. Add 5 tablespoons water. Mix in salt. Cover and cook for 25 minutes over medium-low heat.
5. Prepare garnish: in a separate frying pan, heat vegetable oil on high heat. When hot, add onions and sauté until dark brown but not burned. Set aside.
6. Add lemon juice to chard. Transfer to a serving plate and garnish with browned onions.
7. Serve at room temperature.

Serves 4

Syria
Foul Muqala

Sauteed Fava Beans with Cilantro and Garlic

Ingredients

2 pounds fresh fava beans
4 tablespoons crushed garlic
3 cups minced cilantro
½ cup olive oil
½ cup vegetable oil
2 cups water
¼ cup lemon juice
3 teaspoons salt, divided

Preparation

1. Follow directions for **Green Fava Bean Preparation** in the **Salad Chapter** on page 12.

2. ▲Heat both oils in a large pot on medium-high heat. Add fava beans. Mix in 1 teaspoon salt. Cover pot stirring occasionally.

3. ▲When beans are tender, add garlic. Mix well.

4. ▲Add cilantro. Mix well. Add water to cover. Add lemon juice and remaining 2 teaspoons salt. Cook, covered, on high heat until boiling. Reduce heat to medium, stirring occasionally for 10 minutes. Uncover and cook until most of the water evaporates. The beans should be tender but retain their shape.
5. Serve at room temperature or refrigerate and serve cold.

Serves 4-6

Egg Chapter

Ahmed and the Disappearing Eggs

Hajjah Naziha relates, "When I was around five years old we went to visit my father's family in Cyprus. They had a garden, where they raised chickens and roosters. We used to play with the other children there.

"One of the neighborhood children, named Ahmed was naughty. For example, he used to put water in all the women's shoes who were coming to *dhikr*. Ahmed was also very familiar with the garden and the chickens' habits. He knew when a chicken was laying a fresh egg from the special, loud, crowing sound it made '*bak bak bak*.' He used to ask us to play a game. He said, 'Let's pretend we are making a cake like my aunt does.' He dug a hole in the ground saying, 'This is the flour (the sand around the hole).' Then he said, 'Let's mix eggs into the flour.' He then gathered many eggs and mixed them all in with the dirt.

"Everyone would wait for the eggs in the wintertime especially because in the winter it is very rare to get eggs from the chickens. Ahmad's aunt, the chickens' owner, would hear the chickens telltale squawk, and expect to find fresh-laid eggs, but there were none there.' Eventually, she said, 'My chickens have gone crazy. They make their sound without laying any eggs!'

"Ahmed was a bully so we were afraid to tell his aunt what he had done. I told my mother, though and she told Ahmed's aunt who then put a lock on the chicken coop. This way she was able to save her eggs.

"Oddly enough, Ahmed ended up becoming a successful doctor in Turkey!"

Note: Hajjah Naziha has two ways of preparing certain egg dishes; either in a skillet or transferred to a baking dish and cooked in the oven. Both are equally delicious. The advantage of cooking in the skillet is that you have fewer dishes.

The advantage of cooking in the oven is that you can prepare some other food, or set the table, while the eggs are baking. You can put the dish in the oven and then "forget it" while preparing other dishes. We have presented instructions for both methods where it applies.

Middle East
Hurmalı Yumurta

Eggs and Dates

His Eminence Mawlana Shaykh Nazim ق has performed the Hajj thirty times as of the writing of this cookbook. Many decades ago, when he returned from Hajj, he would bring back blessed dates from Mecca and Medina. He and his family were living in Damascus at the time, and dates were then unavailable in Damascus.

Upon his return, Hajjah Amina ق would prepare this special dish, for him and her family. She would cook the dates in ghee, known as *saman baladi* in Arabic, and then crack eggs over them. She'd cook the dates with eggs for breakfast because Shaykh Nazim likes it very much. She would make Shaykh Nazim his own plate, and then share a plate of the dish with her children.

Ingredients
9 large dates
2 tablespoons butter or *ghee* (clarified butter, available at Middle East stores)
4 eggs
salt (dash)
pepper (dash)

Preparation

1. ▲Cut dates in half. Remove pits from dates.

2. Melt butter or ghee in a medium-size frying pan on high heat.
3. When melted, add dates. Reduce heat to medium.

4. ▲Sauté dates for 2 minutes, or until dates soften a bit.

5. ▲Crack eggs evenly in pan.
6. Sprinkle each egg with a little salt and pepper.
7. Cover skillet and reduce heat to medium. Cook for 3-5 minutes, or until eggs are done.
8. Slide dates and eggs off the skillet and onto a serving plate.
9. Serve hot.

Serves 2-4

Cyprus
Kuşkonmazlı Yumurta

Asparagus Tips and Eggs

Ingredients
3 tablespoons olive oil (can substitute an olive oil spray)
1 bunch asparagus tips
8 eggs
salt (dash)
white pepper (dash)

Preparation

1. ▲In a skillet, heat olive oil over medium-high heat. When hot, add asparagus tips. Sprinkle with salt.
2. Sauté for a minute or until asparagus is wilted.

3. ▲Break whole eggs over asparagus. Sprinkle eggs with salt and white pepper..
4. Cover skillet and reduce heat to medium. Cook for 3-5 minutes, or until eggs are done.
5. Slide asparagus and eggs off the skillet and unto a serving plate.
6. Serve hot.

Serves 4-6

Cyprus
Siyah Zeytinli Yumurta

Fried Eggs with Black Olives

Ingredients
3 tablespoons olive oil
½ cup Middle-Eastern black olives, unpitted
8 eggs
salt (dash)

Preparation

1. ▲ In a skillet, heat olive oil over high heat. When hot, break eggs into skillet. Sprinkle eggs with salt.

2. ▲ Evenly sprinkle olives around eggs.
3. Cover skillet and reduce heat to medium. Cook for 3-5 minute, or until eggs are done.
4. Slide black olives and eggs off the skillet and onto a serving plate.
5. Serve hot.

Serves 4

America

Bird's Nest Eggs

A great dish for kids!

Ingredients
3 slices (loaf) bread
3 eggs
1 tablespoon butter
salt (dash)
pepper (dash)

Preparation

1. ▲ Using a biscuit cutter, make a small hole in the center of each piece of bread.
2. Melt the butter in a frying pan. Place bread in melted butter.

3. ▲ Crack an egg in the hole of each bread slice. Sprinkle with salt and pepper. Cook until golden brown.
4. Turn over and brown other side.
5. Serve hot.

Serves 3 kids or 2 adults.

Cyprus
Hellimli Yumurta

Golden Fried Cheese with Eggs

Ingredients
1 packet Haloum cheese (8 ounces)
4 tablespoons olive oil (or butter)
6 eggs

Preparation

1. ▲ Cut Haloum cheese into ¼-inch slices. They should be rectangular.

2. ▲ Heat olive oil (or melt butter) in a large skillet over medium-high heat. Add Haloum cheese slices and cook until golden brown on the bottom. Flip the cheese over.

3. ▲ Immediately crack the eggs over Haloum cheese slices. The second side of Haloum cheese will brown as it cooks with the eggs. Cover the Haloum cheese and eggs and cook over medium-low heat until eggs are done.
4. Haloum cheese and eggs should be made in a skillet (not in the oven).
5. Serve warm.

Serves 2-3

Cyprus
Mantarlı Yumurta

Sautéed Onions and Mushrooms with Eggs

Ingredients
16 ounces fresh (or 2 8-ounce cans) mushrooms, sliced ¼-inch thick
1 medium onion, finely chopped
3 tablespoons vegetable oil
1 ½ tablespoons olive oil
½ teaspoon salt
1/8 teaspoon black pepper
1/8 teaspoon cinnamon
4 eggs
paprika (dash)

Preparation
1. Preheat oven to 400°F (if cooking in the oven).
2. Heat vegetable and olive oils over high heat in a skillet. Add the onion and sauté until golden brown. Add sliced mushrooms and reduce heat to low. Sauté the onions and mushrooms together until mushrooms are soft. Then sprinkle with salt, pepper and cinnamon.

3. ▲ If cooking in the oven, go to Step 5. If cooking eggs in the skillet, make 4 evenly spaced holes in the mushrooms and onions. Crack an egg into each hole. Sprinkle each egg with a little paprika.

4. Cover and cook over medium-low heat for 10-15 minutes, or until eggs are cooked to your liking. Go to Step 7.
5. Put mushroom mixture in an oven-safe baking dish. Make 4 evenly spaced holes in the mushrooms. Crack an egg into each hole. Sprinkle each egg with a little salt and paprika, to give red color. Cover dish with aluminum foil.
6. Bake, covered, for 15-20 minutes, or until the eggs are cooked to your liking.
7. Serve warm.

Serves 2

Cyprus
Ispanakli Yumurta

Eggs on a Bed of Sautéed Onions and Spinach

Ingredients
1 medium onion, finely chopped
¼ cup olive oil
¼ cup vegetable oil
4 24-ounce packages frozen spinach
1 teaspoon salt
½ teaspoon cinnamon
¼ cup lemon juice
8 eggs
½ teaspoon paprika

Preparation
1. Preheat oven to 400°F (if cooking in the oven).
2. Warm olive and vegetable oils over high heat in a skillet. When oil is hot, add onion and sauté until golden brown.
3. Squeeze spinach very well so that it's not too wet. Add spinach to onion and stir. Stir in salt, cinnamon, and lemon juice. Sauté together for about ten minutes over medium heat.

4. ▲ If cooking in the oven, go to Step 6. If cooking eggs in the skillet, make 8 evenly spaced holes in the spinach mixture.

5. ▲ Crack an egg into each hole.

6. Sprinkle each egg with a little salt and paprika, to give red color. Cover the skillet and cook over medium heat for 3-5 minutes, or until eggs are cooked. Go to Step 9.
7. Put spinach in an oven-safe baking dish. Make 8 evenly spaced holes in the spinach. Crack an egg into each hole. Sprinkle each egg with a little salt and paprika, to give red color. Cover dish with aluminum foil.
8. Bake, covered, for 15-20 minutes, or until the eggs are cooked to your liking.
9. Serve hot.

Serves 4-6

Turkey
Jazmaz

Eggs over Sautéed Vegetables

"Jaz" is the sound food makes when put in hot oil; hence the Turkish name of this filling and nutritious dish. The vegetables are cooked one at a time, and then cooked together with the eggs, resulting in a large casserole of sautéed vegetables, topped with eggs. This can be prepared either in a skillet, or cooked in the skillet and then baked in the oven.

Ingredients

1 large eggplant, peeled and cut into ½-inch cubes
4 medium potatoes, peeled and cut into ½-inch cubes
2 1/8 teaspoons of salt (divided)
1 large zucchini, cut into ½-inch cubes
1 green pepper, cut into ½-inch cubes
1 medium onion, finely chopped
2 plum tomatoes, chopped
1 cup vegetable oil
8 eggs
½ teaspoon black pepper
¼ teaspoon chili pepper (optional)

Preparation

1. Preheat oven to 400°F (if baking in the oven).
2. Set eggplant aside in a large bowl and cover evenly with 1 ½ teaspoons of salt. Let the salted eggplant sit in the bowl for at least ten minutes to draw out any bitter juices.
3. In a fry pan or skillet, warm the vegetable oil over high heat. Add ½ teaspoon of salt to the oil. Add and sauté potatoes until golden brown, stirring occasionally to cook evenly. Remove potatoes with a slotted spoon.
4. Take the eggplant cubes out of their bowl and one handful at a time squeeze the eggplant in your hand, making a fist. A lot of bitter juice will come out into the bowl. Add the squeezed eggplant to the hot oil.
5. Cook the eggplant in the same oil until dark golden brown. Remove with a slotted spoon and put on top of the potatoes. Add zucchini to the oil. Cook zucchini in the same oil until dark golden brown. Remove the zucchini with a slotted spoon and put on top of the potatoes and eggplant.
6. Add green peppers to the oil. Cook the peppers in the same oil until dark golden brown. Remove the green peppers with a slotted spoon and put on top of the rest of the vegetables.
7. Sauté the onion in the oil until light golden brown. Stir constantly so the onions don't burn. Add chopped tomatoes to the onion. Stir in 1/8 teaspoon of salt to soften and draw out the tomato juices.
8. Add reserved cooked potatoes, eggplant, zucchini and green peppers to the tomato-onion mixture.
9. Mix the cooked vegetables very well. Cook over low heat, stirring occasionally for five minutes so the flavors meld together. Stir in black pepper and another ¼ teaspoon of salt.
10. Evenly spread the vegetable mixture on the bottom of the skillet.
11. Make 8 evenly spaced small holes in the mixture. Crack an egg into each hole. Sprinkle each egg with salt and paprika.
12. Cover and cook for 10 minutes, over low heat until the eggs are done to your liking. Go to Step 15.
13. If baking, transfer and spread the cooked vegetables into a baking dish. Make 8 evenly-spaced small holes. Crack an egg into each hole. Sprinkle each egg with salt and paprika.
14. Bake, covered for 15-20 minutes, or until the eggs are done.
15. Serve warm with salad.

Serves 6-8

Cyprus
Pastırmalı Yumurta

Eggs over Savory Cured Meat

Ingredients
4 tablespoons olive oil
7 pieces of *basterma* (*basterma* is a cured meat available in Middle Eastern stores; sold in 1/16-inch thick ovals)
8 eggs
salt (dash)

Preparation
1. Heat olive oil in a large skillet over high heat.
2. When hot, add *basterma* pieces and cook. *Basterma* will sizzle when put in oil.
3. Turn *basterma* pieces upside-down when slightly crispy around edges.

4. ▲ Crack eggs over *basterma*. Sprinkle each egg with a little salt (not too much because the *basterma* itself is salty).
5. Cover skillet and reduce heat to medium-low. Cook, covered, for 3-5 minutes, or until eggs are cooked.

Note: It is important to reduce heat so *basterma* won't dry up and eggs will cook evenly.

6. Slide *basterma* and eggs off the skillet and onto a serving plate.
7. Serve hot, with pita bread and fresh lemon juice.

Serves 3-4

Cyprus
Kıymalı Yumurta

Eggs over Seasoned Ground Beef

Ingredients
1 pound ground beef
1 finely chopped medium onion
1½ teaspoons salt
1 teaspoon pepper
1 teaspoon cinnamon
¼ cup chopped parsley
6 eggs
paprika (dash)

Preparation
1. Preheat oven to 400°F (if baking in the oven).
2. Cook the ground beef and onion over medium heat in a skillet; stirring constantly until brown. Add the salt, pepper and cinnamon. Mix in the parsley and turn off the heat.
3. If cooking in the oven, go to Step 5.
4. If cooking in the skillet, make 6 evenly-spaced holes in ground beef mixture. Crack an egg into each hole. Sprinkle each egg with paprika and salt. Cover and cook over medium-low heat until the eggs are done to your liking. Skip to Step 6.

5. ▲Pour the ground beef mixture into a baking pan. Make 6 evenly-spaced holes in ground beef mixture. Crack an egg into each hole. Sprinkle each egg with paprika and salt. Bake at 400°F uncovered for 15-20 minutes, or until eggs are cooked.
6. Serve hot.

Serves 3-4

Cyprus
Suda Kızartılmış Yumurta

Poached Eggs

H.E. Mawlana Shaykh Nazim's ق favorite breakfast!

Ingredients
4 eggs
1 tablespoon vinegar
Salt (dash)
Pepper (dash)
1 tablespoon fresh lemon juice
1 tablespoon olive oil

Preparation

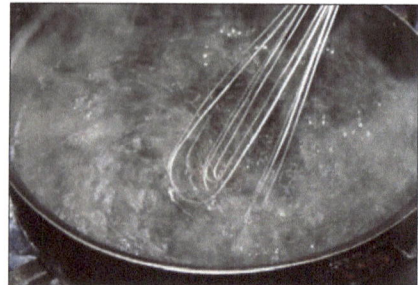

1. ▲ Bring 6 cups of water to a rapid boil in a deep skillet over high heat.
2. Add vinegar to the water.

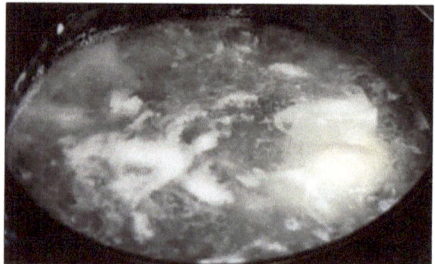

3. ▲ Crack the first egg into the boiling water. Let cook for 2-3 minutes.

4. ▲ Remove egg with a slotted spoon and place on a serving plate. Continue cooking the rest of the eggs the same way, one at a time.
5. Sprinkle with salt and pepper. Evenly sprinkle with fresh lemon juice and olive oil.
6. Serve warm, with bread.

Serves 2-4

Cyprus
Patatesli Yumurta

Eggs Scrambled with Golden Potato Cubes

Ingredients
4 medium potatoes, peeled and cut to 1/3-inch cubes
1 cup vegetable oil + 1 teaspoon
½ teaspoon salt + ¼ teaspoon salt
6 eggs
1/8 teaspoon black pepper

Preparation
1. Put potato cubes in a bowl of water so they won't brown.
2. In a fry pan or skillet, warm vegetable oil over high heat. Add ½ teaspoon of salt to oil. When oil is hot, add potatoes. Fry potatoes until light golden brown, stirring occasionally to cook evenly. Remove potatoes with a slotted spoon.
3. Pour out the oil from the pan, reserving 1 teaspoon of oil to cook the eggs.
4. In a medium bowl, scramble the eggs; add a ¼ teaspoon of salt and the pepper.

5. ▲ Put potatoes back into the pan.
6. Heat and pour scrambled eggs over the potatoes.

7. ▲ Cook until eggs are done.
8. Serve hot.

Serves 4

49

Turkey
Menemen

Onions and Tomatoes Scrambled with Eggs

Ingredients
3 large, soft tomatoes
2 finely chopped medium onions
¼ cup olive oil
1 tablespoon vegetable oil
8 eggs
1 teaspoon salt
¼ teaspoon pepper

Preparation
1. **Peel tomatoes:** Place the tomatoes in a large bowl of hot water. Let sit for 5-10 minutes; then the tomatoes will peel easily.
2. Cut tomatoes into ½-inch cubes. Set aside.
3. Heat olive and vegetable oils over high heat in a skillet. When oil is hot, add onions and sauté until golden. Stir onions constantly so they won't burn. Add chopped tomatoes. Add salt and pepper.

Note: The salt makes the tomatoes soften quickly.

4. Cover and cook for a minute. Uncover and reduce heat to medium to let some of the juice evaporate

5. Whisk eggs in a bowl. Set aside.

6. ▲ Pour eggs over tomatoes and onions in skillet. Cook, stirring constantly over medium-high heat until eggs are done. Keep covered until ready to serve.
7. Serve warm, with bread. This dish is often served in the summer, when tomatoes are plentiful.

Serves 4-6

Lebanon
Maqaaniq bil-Bayd

Small Sausages and Eggs

Ingredients
¾ pound *Makanic* sausages (available at Middle Eastern stores), thinly sliced into ¼-inch rounds

Note: Keep the casing on the *Makanic* sausages while cooking (unlike *Soujuk* sausages for which you remove the casing).

¼ cup corn oil
6 eggs
¼ teaspoon salt

Preparation
1. Warm oil over medium-high heat. When hot, add chopped sausages and cook until dark brown. Be careful not to break the *Makanic* while cooking. If they break when stirred, shake the pan to turn the *Makanic*.
2. Scramble eggs in a medium bowl with salt.
3. Pour scrambled eggs over cooked *Makanic*. Cook on high heat, stirring constantly, until eggs are cooked.

The eggs should absorb the flavor of the *Makanic*; that's why no other spices are added to them.
4. Serve warm.

Serves 4-6

Turkey and Cyprus
Sucuklu Yumurta

Eggs Scrambled with Spicy Sausage Rounds

Ingredients
- ¾ pound Soujuk (the equivalent of one U-shaped "Soujuk" or "Seljuk" sausage available in Middle Eastern stores)
- 8 eggs
- 1 ½ tablespoons olive oil (only needed if you have Soujuk that isn't fatty and doesn't make its own oil; see **Note**)
- ½ teaspoon salt

Preparation
1. **Peel the *Soujuk*:** remove it from the casing with a sharp knife. Slice the *Soujuk* into ¼-inch thick rounds.
2. Heat the oil on high. When hot, add sliced *Soujuk* and reduce the heat to medium.

Note: If the *Soujuk* releases oil when hot, there is no need to add oil. If the *Soujuk* does not release any oil, then add the olive oil.

3. Let cook for 2-3 minutes or until brown on the bottom. Flip the *Soujuk* over to brown other side.
4. Scramble eggs in a medium bowl. Mix in salt. Pour scrambled eggs over the *Soujuk*. Cook over high heat, stirring constantly until eggs are cooked.
5. Serve warm, with lemon juice and bread.

Serves 6-8

Bean Chapter

Openings

Hajjah Naziha said, "I had already closed the book, done. But I re-opened it to add this recipe because my daughter was requesting it a lot." The recipe her daughter, Sajeda, requested is known in Arabic as *foul*. In this chapter it is known as Fava and Garbanzo Bean Spread. A combination of fava and garbanzo beans makes *foul* a healthy dish, rich in protein, fiber and Omega-3's. While taking the picture of the completed dish Hajjah said "*Ya* Saju, this is for you. This book is for you, my daughter." This is the final touch added to the cookbook. Sajeda loves eating this dish with her parents and family.

Sajeda's preference for *foul,* a bean dish, is an example of how people are awakening to a greater variety of healthful foods. Nutritious, inexpensive, and tasty, beans are a wonderful food choice, which more and more people are wisely incorporating into their diet. Garbanzo beans, also known as chick peas, are a staple of Middle Eastern food and any healthy diet. However, people unfamiliar with garbanzo beans, known as *hummous* in Arabic, often shy away from cooking them. Hajjah Naziha encourages you to try them!

Hajjah explains how to cook both dried and canned garbanzo beans in Garbanzo Bean Preparation in this chapter. She soaks the dried beans overnight and then cooks them the following morning. The dry beans are traditionally cooked in a clay or ceramic pot, which lends its own unique flavor to the garbanzos. However, they cook very nicely in modern metal pots as well. A method for improving the taste of canned garbanzo beans is also given. *Sahtein*—to your good health!

Garbanzo Bean Preparation

Method for Preparing Dry Garbanzo Beans

Ingredients
1 cup of dried garbanzo beans - produces 2 ½ cups of cooked garbanzo beans (adjust amount according to recipe)
½ teaspoon baking soda, for soaking.
½ teaspoon baking soda, for boiling.

Preparation

1. ▲ Dissolve baking soda in a large bowl of hot water. Add dry beans. Let sit overnight.

2. In the morning, strain and rinse beans.

3. ▲ Put beans in a soup pot with fresh water. Dissolve baking soda for boiling into pot. Bring to a boil, covered, on high heat. Once the water boils, uncover the pot and reduce the heat to medium. A bubbly white foam will be produced when cooking beans. Spoon off foam and discard.

Note: Removing foam helps remove some of the gaseous properties of the garbanzo beans.

4. Boil beans for 50 minutes, or until tender. Strain and save the water used to cook the garbanzo beans in (if broth is needed in recipe).
5. Use as needed.

Method for Preparing Canned Garbanzo Beans

The alternative to dry beans is canned garbanzo beans (available in almost any grocery store); which are sometimes viewed as having a "tinny" taste. Hajjah knows how to make even canned garbanzo beans taste better.

Ingredients
1 can (14 ½ ounces) garbanzo beans produces 1 ½ cups cooked garbanzo beans (adjust amount according to recipe)

Preparation
1. Strain the canned garbanzo beans and rinse.
2. Put beans in a pot with fresh water, and bring to a boil on high heat. As soon as the water boils, remove from the heat and strain again.

Note: The boiling process removes the tinny taste and also helps remove some of the gaseous properties of the garbanzo beans.
3. Use as needed.

Damascus
Baleela

Garbanzo Bean and Parsley Salad

Ingredients
4 cups cooked garbanzo beans (1 ½ cups dry)
See **Garbanzo Bean Preparation** at beginning of chapter, page 54.
1 teaspoon cumin
Olive oil (to drizzle on top)
1 tablespoon salt
1 tablespoon finely chopped garlic
¼ cup lemon juice
½ cup olive oil

Garnish
2 teaspoons finely chopped parsley

Preparation
1. Place garbanzo beans in medium-sized bowl. Stir in salt, garlic, lemon juice and olive oil.
2. Garnish with parsley and cumin. Drizzle with olive oil.
3. Serve at room temperature.

Serves 4

Lebanon
Hummus bis-Snawbaar

Buttery Pine Nuts and Garbanzo Beans

Hajjah Naziha's mother-in-law, Hajjah Yousra, would often prepare this dish, usually eaten at brunch as a savory side dish or *mezze*. A hearty dish, wonderful to serve on winter mornings with warm pita bread.

Ingredients
4 tablespoons butter
¼ cup pine nuts
3 cups cooked garbanzo beans (1 ¼ cups dry)
See **Garbanzo Bean Preparation** at beginning of chapter, page 54.
½ teaspoon salt (adjust to taste)

Preparation
1. Melt butter in a small saucepan on medium heat. Sauté pine nuts until golden brown, stirring constantly so they don't burn. Remove from heat.
2. Place garbanzo beans in a shallow bowl. Mix in salt. Pour pine nuts and butter over the beans.
3. Serve warm with pita bread and cucumber pickles.

Serves 2-4

Lebanon
Fattat Hummus bil-Labn ma` at-Taheena

Garbanzo Beans in Yogurt and Tahini

Hajjah Naziha learned from her blessed mother, Hajjah Amina(ق) many ways to avoid waste. This dish is a great way to use up old bread which is going stale! You can use pita bread or substitute a different type of bread.

Ingredients
3-4 thin pita loaves
5 cups cooked garbanzo beans (1 ½ cups dry) + 4 ½ cups reserved cooking broth
See **Garbanzo Bean Preparation** at beginning of chapter, page 54.
4 cloves crushed garlic
4 teaspoons salt
3 tablespoons *tahini* (available at Middle Eastern stores)
2 pounds + 1 cup plain yogurt
1 tablespoon lemon juice (optional)

Note: Lebanese yogurt is tarter than American yogurt, so this tastes more authentically Middle Eastern with lemon juice mixed into the yogurt. If you prefer milder foods, omit the lemon juice.

Garnish
¼ cup butter
¼ cup pine nuts (optional)
1 teaspoon chili powder or paprika (optional)
¼ cup chopped parsley

Preparation

1. ▲ Tear pita bread into small pieces. Broil in oven until well-toasted; brown and crispy. Place at bottom of a serving dish.
2. Prepare sauce for bread: mix 4 ½ cups of reserved garbanzo bean broth, crushed garlic and salt. Pour evenly over bread.
3. Mix 4 ½ cups of garbanzo beans into bread, reserve ½ cup of garbanzos for garnish.
4. Mix *tahini*, yogurt and lemon juice in a bowl.
5. Spread *tahini* and yogurt mixture over garbanzo beans and bread.
6. Garnish with reserved ½ cup of garbanzo beans.
7. Melt butter in a small saucepan. Add pine nuts and chili powder to butter and sauté until golden brown.
8. Pour seasoned butter evenly over yogurt. Garnish with chopped parsley.
9. Serve immediately! This dish should be made just before serving so it is eaten hot and the bread does not become soggy.

Serves 6-8

Lebanon
Fattat bit-Taheena

Crispy Bread Smothered with Garbanzo Beans and Tahini

Ingredients
3-4 pita loaves
5 cloves chopped garlic, divided
¾ cup lemon juice
¾ cup *tahini* (available at Middle Eastern stores)
4 ½ cups cooked garbanzo beans (1 ¾ cups dry) + 3 cups reserved cooking broth, divided
See **Garbanzo Bean Preparation** at beginning of chapter, page 54.
2 teaspoons salt

Garnish
¼ cup butter
¼ cup pine nuts

Preparation

1. ▲ Tear pita bread into small pieces. Broil until well-toasted, brown and crispy. Place at bottom of a serving dish.
2. **Prepare *hummous* in a food processor or blender**: mix 2 cloves of the garlic with lemon juice and *tahini*. Mix in ½ cup of the reserved garbanzo bean broth. Put 3 ½ cups of the garbanzo beans in food processor. Blend until smooth. Add another 1/3 cup of garbanzo broth and blend until smooth.
3. **Prepare sauce for bread**: mix salt with 2 cups of chick pea broth in a bowl. Mix in remaining 2 cloves of crushed garlic. Pour evenly over top of bread.
4. Spread *hummous* over bread.
5. Garnish with remaining one cup of garbanzo beans.
6. Melt butter in a small saucepan. Sauté pine nuts until golden brown. Sprinkle over garbanzo beans.
7. Serve warm, immediately.

Serves 4-6

Lebanon
Hummous bil-Lahma Mafrouma

Garbanzo Beans and Tahini with Ground Beef Topping

Ingredients
5 cups cooked garbanzo beans (2 cups dry) + 1 cup reserved cooking broth
See **Garbanzo Bean Preparation** at beginning of chapter, page 54.
¾ cup lemon juice
3 cloves garlic
1 teaspoon salt
½ cup tahini
½ teaspoon cumin powder
½ teaspoon chili powder or paprika
½ bunch parsley (½ cup)
3 teaspoons olive oil

Ground Beef Topping
1 small onion
½ pound ground beef
1 teaspoon salt
½ teaspoon pepper
½ teaspoon cinnamon
2 tablespoons butter
¼ cup pine nuts

Preparation
1. Place garbanzo beans in a blender or food processor fitted with the metal blade; blend until smooth. Add reserved cooking broth, lemon juice, crushed garlic, salt and tahini. Blend until hummous is the consistency of a paste.
2. Transfer to a shallow serving dish.
3. Prepare meat topping: Finely chop onion and brown with ground beef over medium heat. Add salt, pepper and cinnamon.
4. In a saucepan, melt butter; stirring frequently, sauté pine nuts until golden brown. Add sautéed pine nuts and butter to meat mixture and cook together for a couple of minutes.
5. Spread meat mixture on top of prepared *hummos*.
6. Serve at room temperature.

Serves 6-8

Lebanon
Foul

Fava and Garbanzo Bean Spread

Ingredients

▲ 4 cups dried fava beans.

▲ 2 cups dried chick peas.
1 teaspoon baking soda, divided for soaking.
1 teaspoon baking soda, divided for boiling.
Note: The baking soda helps reduce gas and helps the beans cook faster.
1 teaspoon cumin
4-5 cloves garlic (1 tablespoon crushed)
1 ½ cups lemon juice (preferably freshly squeezed)
1 ¼ cup olive oil
1 ½ tablespoons salt (or to taste)

Garnish
½ cup chickpeas (reserved from the 2 cups boiled)
½ cup olive oil
½ cup chopped parsley

Preparation
8. Place beans in separate bowls and cover with water, so the water is about 2 ½ inches above the beans. Add ½ teaspoon baking soda to each bowl. Soak overnight.

9. ▲ Drain beans in the morning. Place beans in two separate pots. (one for fava and one for chick peas). Add enough water in each pot to cover beans by three inches. Add ½ teaspoon baking soda to each pot.
10. Boil on high, skimming foam from

top of beans. Boil the fava beans 30-40 minutes.

Note: Cooking times vary by age of beans. Keep checking if ready so the beans don't become mushy. As soon they are tender to bite they are done. Remove immediately from water.

11. ▲ Drain immediately, so they do not become soupy. Set aside in strainer over a bowl.

12. ▲ Boil the chick peas for about 30 minutes. Keep checking if ready.

See **Garbanzo Bean Preparation** at beginning of chapter, page 54. Strain immediately and set aside in a colander with a bowl under it.

13. ▲ Combine both beans together in a large bowl. Reserve ½ cup of the chick peas for the garnish.

14. ▲ Mash the beans with a mortar or potato masher until half the beans are mashed and half the beans are still whole.

15. Crush the garlic. Combine with olive oil, lemon juice, cumin and salt

Note: The cumin is for flavor and to take gas away from the beans.

16. ▲ Pour this dressing into the mashed beans. Stir to combine well. Adjust seasoning to taste.

17. Place in a serving bowl and garnish with reserved ½ cup of chick peas and parsley. Pour the ½ cup olive oil over it in a decorative way.

18. Serve warm or at room temperature.

19. Serve with pita bread, white onions, green onions, radishes, pickles and sliced vegetables.

Serves 5-10

Southeastern Turkey
Mercimekli Kısır

Spicy Vegetarian Lentil Patties

Ingredients
1 cup red lentils
3 cups water
2 ½ cups bulgur
1/3 cup olive oil
1 finely chopped small onion
2 tablespoons tomato paste
1-2 tablespoons hot chili, fresh or powder
6 thinly sliced green onions
½ cup finely chopped parsley
2 teaspoons cumin
1 ½ teaspoons salt
½ teaspoon pepper

Preparation
1. Rinse lentils and drain.
2. Put lentils and water in a small soup pot. Bring to a boil over high heat. Reduce heat to medium-low and continue to boil uncovered, for 10-15 minutes, or until lentils are cooked and soft.

3. ▲ Add bulgur to lentils; stir and cover the pot. Shut off heat and leave on stove for at least 15 minutes; this will cook the bulgur partially. If bulgur is still watery, push bulgur aside from edge of pot, so there is a fist-sized hole at edge of pot. Add another 1/3 cup bulgur into the hole. Cover new bulgur with cooked bulgur. Smooth down. Cover pot to let bulgur absorb water. Let sit for 10 more minutes, or until bulgur has absorbed water.
4. Meanwhile, heat olive oil in a frying pan over medium-high heat. When hot, add chopped onion and sauté until soft and transparent. Add tomato paste and chili. Mix well. Turn off heat.

5. ▲ Put lentils and bulgur into the tomato paste mixture. Mix and leave to cool.
6. Once mixture has cooled, mix in green onion, parsley, cumin, salt, and pepper.

7. ▲ Take about ¼ cup of the mixture and form into 3-inch, oblong, finger-shaped patties.
8. Place patties on a serving dish. Serve with olive oil for dipping.
9. Serve cold or at room temperature.

Serves 4

Bread Chapter

Significance of Wheat Grains and Bread

The following ayat from Surah al-Baqarah demonstrates the sustainability of grains such as wheat and corn. These grains have a remarkable ability to produce several hundred grains from one.

> *The parable of those who spend what they own in the name of Allah is that of a grain: It grows seven ears, and each ear has a hundred grains. Allah gives increase many times over to whom He pleases; and Allah is Enough, All Knowing (2:261).*

Likewise the following ayat from Surah Yusuf shows the importance of grain in times of a food shortage.

> *(Yusuf) said: 'For seven consecutive years you shall carefully sow (and grow) as you are used to (doing): And the crops that you reap, you will leave them in the ear – Except a little, from which you will eat (12:47).*

This is a well known reference to wheat in which *Sayyidina* Yusuf ﷺ instructs the Egyptian people to save wheat for the predicted period of drought as foretold in the king's dream. He ﷺ told the Egyptian people to preserve the wheat for later use by leaving the grains uncrushed in their stems.

Both of these verses indicate the vital importance of grains in the daily diet of humankind.

The holy Prophet ﷺ himself used to eat barley bread with vinegar and oil for dinner every day. Therefore it is not surprising that this reliance on grains stretches back to the parents of humanity.

Hajjah Naziha relates, "*Sayyidina* Adam ﷺ and *Sayyiditina* Hawa (Eve) ﷺ were expelled from Paradise because they ate from the tree. When they arrived to Earth, they felt hungry. Archangel Gabriel ﷺ came and showed them how to plant, harvest, and grind wheat. He then showed them how to make fire and bake bread. Miraculously, he showed them all this in just three hours. For this reason, bread is the most basic food to humanity, and people everywhere live off of it and love to eat it.

"Together they made three loaves of bread; two were given to Adam ﷺ and one was given to Eve ﷺ. Eve ﷺ ate half *her* loaf and saved the rest for later, while Adam ﷺ ate all of his bread at once. Eve knew to save food for later. This shows that women, the daughters of Eve, are naturally talented at management of resources and planning for the future."

Hajjah continues, "My mother always kept the house well stocked with flour. Guests would often come unexpectedly to visit my father in the morning. My mother would use the flour to quickly prepare dough for *burek*. She would roll the dough out with an *oklava* (a long rolling pin) and fill the dough with meat or cheese. It was my job to fry the filled dough in oil. Together we would serve the fresh *burek* to guests, within an hour of their arrival. I helped her in the kitchen from when I was nine or ten years old; that's what we did together. Watching her and helping her helped me in my later life because I became very quick in the kitchen. To this day I can form, roll, and cook dough very quickly."

Whole wheat bread is nutritious and filling; it has carbohydrates, protein, and fiber. Whether dipped in tea to fill an empty stomach or served alongside food, bread is essential for human survival. It is only fitting that an angel of God showed the father and mother of humankind how to make this blessed food; a food which He references repeatedly in His Holy Book.

Cyprus
Zeytinli Pide

Savory Black Olive Bread

Mawlana Shaykh Nazim's Olive Bread

The Holy Qur'an refers to olive trees, *"We grow for you ... a tree springing out of Mount Sinai, which produces oil, and relish for those who use it for food."* 23:19-20

As wheat, olive trees, and olive oil are mentioned in the Qur'an, it is suitable that His Eminence Mawlana Shaykh Nazim ف always asks, "Where is my olive bread?"

This traditional Cypriot bread is eaten all year round. It is taken on picnics or for lunch by farmers and gardeners. You won't believe how tasty it is, as well as nutritious.

Please make sure the yeast is fresh, to ensure your dough will rise properly. This is traditionally baked in a circular aluminum baking dish. However, if you don't have one, any baking dish will work (as long as it has sides), a 9x13-inch aluminum baking pan worked well for us. Also, as you will be working with yeast, make sure your kitchen is warm; the yeast needs a temperate environment to rise properly.

A variation of this bread is prepared with Halloum cheese; please see note at the end of the recipe.

Ingredients

2 ½ cups water
6 teaspoons yeast
6 cups flour
2 teaspoons sugar
2 cups black Middle Eastern "dried" olives; 1 ½ cups when pitted (These have very little brine compared to other olives. They are available at Middle Eastern stores, or some health food stores.)
4 medium onions, finely chopped
4 tablespoons dried mint
1 cup olive oil
2-3 tablespoons olive oil (to grease baking pan)

Preparation

1. Warm water until between 110-120 degrees. **Use a thermometer** to ensure water is the right temperature. (This is very important because if the water is too hot it will "kill" the yeast and if the water is too cold the yeast won't activate. Either way, the bread won't rise.)

2. ▲ Mix yeast and sugar into the water, preferably in a ceramic bowl. Mix well for a few minutes, until the yeast is dissolved. Cover bowl with plastic wrap and let sit for 15 minutes. The yeast mixture should rise and foam.

64

3. ▲ In a separate large bowl, add flour. Add yeast mixture to the flour and knead. The dough will soften as you continue to knead it. With your fingers, scrape any remaining ingredients from the sides of the bowl and knead into the dough mixture.

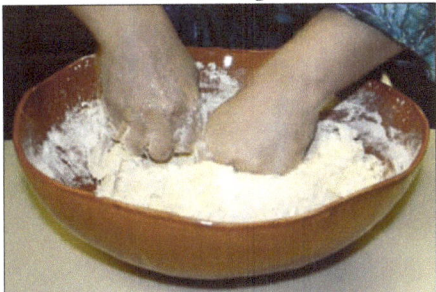

4. ▲ Keep kneading by hand for 5-10 minutes.

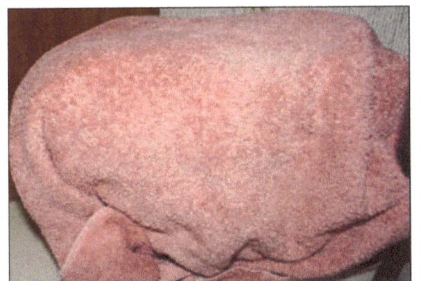

5. ▲ Once the dough forms into a ball, cover bowl with plastic wrap (covering it this way traps the air inside and creates a good environment for the dough to rise) and layer 6 kitchen towels over the plastic wrap and around the bowl to keep the dough warm. If your kitchen is cool, place more towels around sides of bowl to keep it warm. Place bowl in a warm place where there is no draft, like in the corner of the kitchen. Let rise for 1 ½ hours, or until dough doubles in size.

6. Pit olives: Squeeze olives from the top. The top will split open to remove the pit. The olive will be in a "V" shape; open from the top. Discard pits. **Note:** These olives are different from conventional black olives; they are much easier to pit.

7. In a medium mixing bowl add: olives, onion, mint, and olive oil. Mix well.

8. ▲ Pour olive mixture over dough in large bowl. Knead ingredients into dough for 5 minutes.

9. ▲ Knead well, so the ingredients are very well-mixed. Punch dough to mix in ingredients. The dough will become very pliable and elastic.

10. The additional ingredients will "shock" the dough. Thus, the dough needs to rise again before baking. Let rise in the baking dish you are going to use. If dough rises in the bowl and is transferred to a baking dish, it will deflate the dough.

11. Grease baking dish, such as a 9x13-inch aluminum pan with 2-3 tablespoons olive oil.

Note: Make sure the baking dish is warm before you put the dough in it.

12. ▲ Place dough in baking dish and pat down gently to fill sides. Cover dish with plastic wrap and layer the 6 towels over the plastic wrap and around the baking dish. Again place back in a warm place. Let rise for 1 ½ hours, or until dough doubles in size again.

13. Meanwhile, preheat oven to 375°F.

14. Remove plastic wrap. Place bread dough in preheated oven in middle-lower rack. Bake for 1 hour – 1 hour and 15 minutes, or until top is golden. Test for doneness by inserting a knife. If knife comes out clean, bread is done.

Note: When bread is cooked, cover with a towel. Do not cover immediately with aluminum foil because the foil will make the bread soggy.

15. Serve warm or at room temperature.

Serves 6-10

Variation: Halloum Cheese Bread Hallimli bit-ta

Another traditional Cypriot bread is this variation, prepared with Halloum cheese rather than black olives. Halloum cheese is available at Middle Eastern markets and most health food grocery stores. Halloum cheese is unique in so far as it stays in chunks even when it is baked; it does not melt into the bread as other cheeses do.

Substitute 2 packages (approximately 8 ounces each Halloum). Cut into 1/3-inch cubes for the olives in the above recipe. The result is an exceptionally moist and delicious bread.

Russia
Tukmaç Eriştesi

Fettuccini Noodles

Hajjah Amina's mother, Hajjah A'isha, used this dough, from her native Russia, in a wide variety of recipes. She used it in chicken and meat soups, and even in certain desserts.

In Hajjah A'isha's time, she would make the noodles and dry them on large sheets over a 3-4 day period. Once the noodles were dry, she would store them in a small pillowcase with a tie at the top. This was before there were freezers. Now, you can make the noodles and freeze the excess without drying.

Ingredients
2 ½ cups flour
3 eggs
½ teaspoon salt
¼ cup water

Preparation

2. Place dough on a floured surface and knead for approximately 5 minutes. Place back into bowl, cover with a towel. Let sit for 15 minutes.

1. ▲Put flour, eggs, and salt in a bowl. Kneading by hand, slowly add a little water at a time, until a ball of dough forms.

3. ▲Divide dough into 3 equal parts.

4. ▲On a floured surface, roll out the first third of dough with a rolling pin to approximately 1/16- inch thick.

▲ Sprinkle dough with a lot of flour. Roll dough around the rolling pin. The dough will form 2 ½ layers around the rolling pin.

5. ▲ Cut the rolled up dough lengthwise along the rolling pin.

6. ▲ Let the dough come down from the sides of the rolling pin. You will be left with a rectangle of dough. Cut in half lengthwise again.

7. ▲ Place one of the halves of cut dough on top of the other half. Cut the layered dough in half, lengthwise.

8. ▲ Sprinkle more flour on top of one of the cut dough halves.

9. ▲ Place un-floured half on top of the floured half. You will be left with many layers of dough piled on top of each other. Thinly slice pile of noodles cross-wise.

10. ▲ Continue to thinly slice noodles cross-wise until all dough is cut. The noodles should be about 2 inches long.
11. Separate and place noodles on a well-floured tray until ready to use. Separate cut noodles by hand, again sprinkling with flour to keep them separate. Use noodles as needed. Some recipes call for a third of the amount of noodles made. If freezing go to **Step 13** before use, shake the floured noodles in a fine mesh colander to remove excess flour.
12. To freeze the noodles sprinkle them with extra flour in step 12.

Note: The flour will help keep the noodles separate when they are stored and help absorb the moisture.

13. Let floured noodles dry 1-2 hours.
14. Place in zip lock bags and freeze.

Bosnia
Bosna Böreği

Bosnian Burek

Ingredients

Phyllo Dough
6 cups flour
1 tablespoon salt
1 tablespoon oil
2 cups water
3 tablespoons butter, melted

Filling
5 pounds potatoes, about 14 medium- sized potatoes
5 medium onions, separated
2 tablespoons salt, divided
2 teaspoons pepper, divided
2 ¼ pounds ground beef

Topping
½ cup water
1 tablespoon butter
1/8 teaspoon salt

Preparation
1. Preheat oven to 375°F.

2. ▲ **Prepare dough:** Start by making a mound of flour, with a hole in the middle. Pour the salt and olive oil in the center.
3. Start kneading by hand, slowly adding the water, until a large ball of dough forms. Knead for five minutes.

4. ▲ Separate the dough into three smaller balls of dough of equal size. Leave covered. Let rest for at least 1 hour in a warm place.

5. Peel the potatoes and grate them directly into a bowl of water (This prevents the potatoes from turning black).
6. Grate the onions. Mix ground beef, ½ of the grated onions, 1 tablespoon of the salt and 1 teaspoon of the pepper in a separate bowl. Divide into three equal portions while in the bowl for later use.
7. Empty the potatoes into a strainer. Mix in the remaining ½ of the grated onions, 2 teaspoons of the salt and 1 teaspoon of the pepper. Mix well in the strainer. This will season the potatoes and draw the excess water out. Divide into three equal portions while in the strainer for later use.

8. ▲ Lightly flour counter surface. Place one of the three dough balls on floured surface. Sprinkle top of dough ball with flour.

9. ▲ Roll out dough with a long thin rod or a rolling pin.

10. ▲ Continue to roll out dough until 1/16- inch thick.

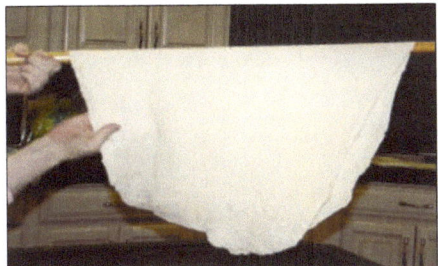

11. ▲ Place dough over the length of the rod. Lift the rolling pin. Using your hand, slowly pull the dough, starting in the middle (where the dough is thickest) and pulling gently out to edges. The dough will become very thin, so thin it will be transparent.

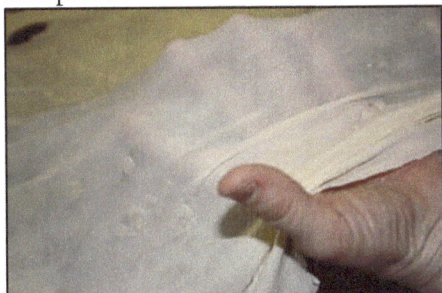

12. ▲ Place dough back down on the counter or on a table. Pull the dough gently towards you from all sides. This will make the dough even thinner. The dough will become as thin as Phyllo dough (thin pasty dough). If the dough tears, do not worry. It will be hidden when you later roll and coil the dough.

13. ▲ Cut flattened dough in half. Sprinkle a little of the melted butter over each half of the dough.

14. ▲ Take a handful of potatoes and squeeze out excess water. Spread potatoes over dough in the shape of a crescent moon; half of the potato mixture on each dough piece. Next sprinkle one half of the meat over the potatoes.

15. ▲ Fold the edges of the dough over the potato and meat filling to cover.

16. ▲ Sprinkle a little more of the melted butter over the folded dough.
17. Start to roll the dough. Gently push dough forward. Your hands should start on the table and carefully push the dough until it starts to form a roll.
18. Start rolling with your hands in the center of the dough. Roll from center all the way to one side. Return to center and roll up other side.

19. ▲ Continue pushing the filled dough over and over to form a roll. Always start rolling the dough in the middle, and slowly roll out to the one side and then the other. Continue rolling, until it is one long roll.

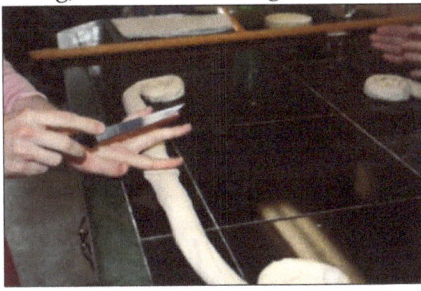

20. ▲ On each end of the roll start coiling the ends like a cinnamon roll. Cut in the middle; first marking halfway with your finger. One half of the dough makes 2 coils.

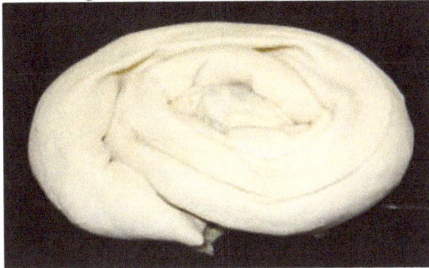

21. ▲ Continue to roll. Make coils until dough is finished. Place coils in baking pan or on cookie sheet. Coat the bottom of a large wide baking pan or cookie sheet with 1 tablespoon olive oil. Alternatively you can use two smaller pans (9x13-inch) with one teaspoon olive oil for 6 coils on each pan. Sprinkle remaining melted butter on each of the coils.
22. Bake for 1 hour.
23. Prepare topping: Bring water, butter and salt to a boil in a pot on high heat. Evenly sprinkle topping over each coil. Place back in the oven for 5-10 minutes.
24. Serve warm, with yogurt. Makes 12 coils.

Serves 6-8.

Russia
Peeramich

Savory Russian Meat Pastries

Hajjah Amina ق, Hajjah Naziha's mother, often made these *peeramich*, or meat pastries from her native Russia. They are unbelievably tasty.

Hajjah Amina ق learned how to make the *peeramich* from her mother, Hajjah A'isha, and would prepare them for her family for dinner. Hajjah Naziha remembers helping her holy mother cook them. Hajjah Amina would have Hajjah Naziha fry the pastries. She taught her to fry them face down, with the meat-side down, while spooning the hot oil over them. Spooning the hot oil like this makes them puffy.

One would think the meat would fall out of the open pastries, but the meat doesn't come out. When the area on the bottom becomes dark golden; you turn it over. When it is turned and the meat filling is face-up, you do not spoon the oil over the top.

This is a great dish to make with someone else; as it is a lot of work. Hajjah Amina ق would have Hajjah Naziha and her sister, Hajjah Ruqayyah, fry the pastries. Hajjah Naziha recommends making it with your children, your husband (!), or your friend(s).

When they are finished, they are served with vinegar.

Ingredients
2 1/4 teaspoons yeast + ½ cup warm water
Note: Fast-rising yeast can also be used, and then change the time it takes for the dough to rise accordingly.
3 cups flour
¾ cup water
1 ½ teaspoons salt
2 cups corn oil for frying + ½ teaspoon salt (so oil doesn't splatter)

Serve with ¼ cup white vinegar mixed with ¼ cup balsamic vinegar.

Filling Ingredients
½ pound ground beef
1 small finely chopped onion
½ teaspoon salt
¼ teaspoon pepper

Preparation

1. ▲ Mix yeast into ½ cup of warm water; between 110 and 120 degrees.

Dissolve yeast in warm water, stirring with a teaspoon.

2. While yeast is sitting in water, run a large mixing bowl under hot water. When the bowl is warm; dry bowl. Mix flour and salt in bowl.

3. Knead the yeast and water into the flour mixture by hand. Slowly add another ¾ cup of warm water. Keep kneading. The dough will form. This dough will be quite elastic (much more elastic than bread dough). Place bowl in a warm spot; covered with a towel. Let sit in a warm place for an hour and a half, or until the dough doubles.

Note: If using fast-rising yeast; the doubling will take about twenty minutes.

5. ▲ Knead the dough slightly with your fingertips to form a small ping-pong size ball, about 2-inches in diameter.

9. ▲ **Fill dough circles:** Place a flat tablespoon of filling in center of circle. Slightly flatten meat filling so that it forms a circle of meat within the circle of dough. There should be 1-inch between the edge of the meat and the edge of the dough.

4. ▲ Form dough to make the pastries: dip a ¼-cup measuring cup or a tablespoon into a bowl of warm water. (Dip the cup or spoon into water so that it won't stick to the dough.) Scoop a flat measuring cup or spoon a heaping tablespoon of the dough. Place onto a floured surface.

6. ▲ Continue until all the dough is formed into balls. Cover the formed balls with a towel.

7. The bowl dough should produce 12-15 balls of dough altogether.

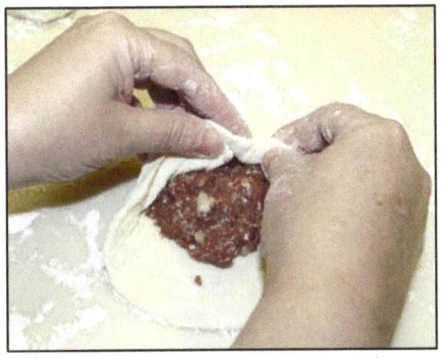

10. ▲ Form the filled pastries: pick up a piece of the dough from the side, and then pick up the piece of dough right next to it. Pinch the two pieces together.

11. ▲ Keep picking up the edge pieces of the dough.

Note: Do not over flour the surface and dust the pastry of excess flour when you are done forming it. If there is too much flour on the surface of the pastry it (the excess flour) will burn when cooking in the oil and turn the oil black so all the subsequent pastries will also look burnt. These pastries are still edible although they look darkened. If the oil becomes very black, pour the oil into a clean pot. The black sediment will settle at the bottom of the pot and you will be able to pour off the clean oil. Discard sediment.

8. ▲ Start forming the pastries: Take a dough ball. Flatten with your hand until it forms a circle approximately 4-5 inches in diameter. Press harder around the edges of the dough circle, so that the outside edges of the circle are a little thinner than the center.

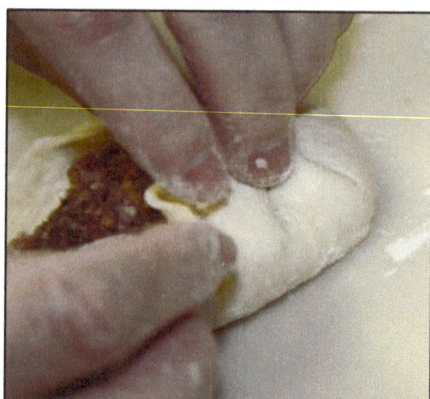

12. ▲Turn the dough as you pick up the edge pieces.

13. ▲There will be a small open circle of meat filling; approximately ½-inch in diameter, at the top.

14. In the end, it will look like a flower; with the pastry in pleats around the meat center.
15. Meanwhile, heat oil in a large pan or wok.. Add ½ teaspoon of salt to oil to prevent splattering. When the oil is hot; add the dough "flowers;" face down.

16. ▲Fry four or five at a time. Keep spooning oil over the top, to make the pastry fluffy, for five minutes. Even though the meat is facing down, the meat will not come out.

17. ▲When bottom of the pastries becomes dark golden, flip over, and cook for three more minutes on the other side. When you cook the other side, don't spoon oil over the top.
18. As they cook; transfer to a covered serving dish in a warm oven.
19. Serve hot (with meat sides up!), with vinegar. Place a spoonful of vinegar into the center, where the meat filling shows.

Serves 6-8

Turkey
Mercimekli Lazanya

Lentil Lasagna

Ingredients
½ cup red lentils
1 cup water
10 lasagna noodles
½ pound ground beef
1 medium onion, finely chopped
1 teaspoon salt
½ teaspoon pepper
½ teaspoon cinnamon
½ cup cooked garbanzo beans

Sauce
3 cups milk
3 tablespoons flour
½ teaspoon salt
1 tablespoon butter
1 cup grated cheddar cheese

Preparation
1. Preheat oven to 350°F.
2. Rinse lentils.
3. To a small saucepan, add one cup of water and lentils. Bring to a boil over high heat. When water boils, reduce heat to medium-high and continue to boil uncovered for 5 minutes, or until lentils are soft.
4. Transfer lentils and their water to a blender and blend until smooth.
5. In a soup pot, bring water to a boil over high heat. When water boils, add lasagna noodles and cook until al dente (follow cook time on lasagna package). When noodles are done, strain and rinse under cold water.
6. **To a fry pan add:** meat, onions, salt, pepper, and cinnamon. Brown meat over medium-high heat. When meat is cooked, mix in garbanzo beans. Stir in blended lentils. Mix well. Set aside.
7. **Prepare sauce:** in a bowl whisk milk, flour and salt. Mix well. In a large saucepan, melt butter. Stirring constantly with a whisk, pour milk mixture into butter. Stir in cheddar cheese. As soon as it starts to thicken, turn off heat but keep on the stove, stirring constantly until it reaches a pudding-like consistency.
8. Take ½ cup of milk sauce and spread it evenly over bottom of a 7x11-inch baking dish.

9. ▲ Lay flat 4 or 5 noodles over the sauce. Then evenly spread all of the meat mixture over the first layer of pasta. Take remaining pasta and put another layer on top of the meat. Using a ladle, spoon remaining sauce evenly over pasta.
10. Bake 45 minutes uncovered, until top is a nice golden brown.
11. Serve hot.

Serves 4-6

Turkey
Peynirli Ravioli

Cheese-Filled Ravioli

Ingredients
Dough
3 cups flour
2 eggs
1 teaspoon salt
2 tablespoons lemon juice
1/3 cup water
3 tablespoons olive oil

Filling
½ cup ricotta cheese
1 teaspoon dried dill
2 tablespoons chopped parsley
4 ounces chopped Feta cheese

Sauce
2 tablespoons butter
2 tablespoons olive oil
1 onion, finely chopped
2 large chopped tomatoes
2 tablespoons tomato paste
2 chopped garlic cloves
3 chopped bell peppers (assorted colors)
2 chopped button mushrooms
1 teaspoon salt
1 teaspoon rosemary
1 teaspoon dried basil
2 tablespoons milk

For Cooking Ravioli
8 cups water
2 tablespoons olive oil
2 teaspoons salt
Parmesan cheese (sprinkle on top)

Preparation
1. **Prepare dough**: mix flour and salt in a large bowl. Make a hole in the flour and place the eggs, lemon juice, and olive oil inside. Start to knead by hand. Slowly add water until a ball of dough forms.

2. ▲ This will be a very stiff, crumbly dough; there is a lot of flour in it. Thus, knead on an unfloured surface; *do not add water.*

3. ▲ Knead dough and it will come together in a ball, after 10-15 minutes.

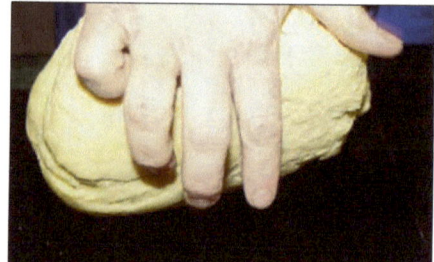

4. ▲ Once ball forms, keep kneading until it becomes smooth. Set aside to rest, covered in a bowl, for at least 10 minutes.

5. **Meanwhile, prepare filling**: mix ricotta cheese, dill, parsley, and feta cheese in a separate bowl. Mix well, until a pasty consistency, like cream. Set aside.

6. ▲Roll dough out until it is 1/16-inch thick.

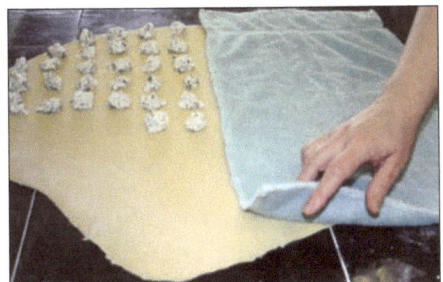

7. ▲Place 1 teaspoon of filling every 2 inches along bottom half of the dough. Once you have finished the filling, fold the second half of dough over the filled half, covering the filling with the dough.

8. ▲Press with your fingers to form a seal along the edges of the dough. Then press your fingers between each bump that you see to form a square. Once you have pressed around all the filling, take a pastry wheel or pizza cutter and cut the dough into squares. Set on a tray with a towel over it so as not to dry out.

9. **Prepare sauce**: melt butter and add olive oil in a large pan on high heat. Once hot, add onions and sauté until soft and clear. Add tomatoes, tomato paste, garlic, peppers and mushrooms. Sauté until soft. Add salt, rosemary, and basil. Cook for about 20 minutes over medium-low heat. Add the milk. Mix well.

10. To a large soup pot add water, salt, and olive oil. Bring to a boil over high heat. Add ravioli. Cook for approximately 10-15 minutes, or until the raviolis float.
11. When the pasta is done, remove with a slotted spoon (reserve pasta water). Place on a serving dish.
12. Stir into sauce: 1 cup of the pasta water. Spoon sauce over pasta. Sprinkle parmesan cheese over sauce.
13. Serve hot.

Serves 6-8

Daghestan
Khinkal

Ground Beef Filled Dumplings in Broth

Ingredients
Dough
3 cups flour, sifted
1 egg
1 cup water
½ teaspoon salt

Ground Beef Filling
1 pound ground beef
1 small onion, finely chopped
2 teaspoons salt
1 teaspoon pepper

Broth
12 cups water
Salt to taste

Sauce #1
3-7 cloves garlic, crushed
1 cup yogurt

Sauce #2
¾ cup vinegar
3-7 cloves garlic, crushed
¼ cup broth used for cooking dumplings

Preparation
1. **Prepare dough**: To a medium bowl add flour and salt. Mix well. Make a shallow hole in the middle.

2. ▲ Break the egg in the hole. Add water to the egg. Mix well with your hands until it forms a ball.
3. Prepare a floured surface **and knead dough:** Fold dough in from the far side towards you and push away from you. Keep taking far side and folding towards you, pushing it away with the heal of your hand. Knead dough until it feels as soft as an earlobe.

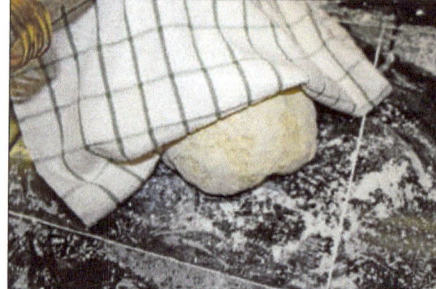

4. ▲ Cover dough with a towel or bowl and let rest for 10 minutes.
5. Remove dough and divide into 2 equal pieces. Cover with a towel. Allow dough to rest for another 5-10 minutes.

6. ▲ **Prepare filling:** To a bowl add ground beef, onion, salt and pepper. Mix well.

7. Take one piece of the dough (keep other covered with kitchen towel). Knead slightly and roll out to a 1/16-inch round.

8. ▲ Cut dough into circles 3.75 inches in diameter using a glass or biscuit cutter. Use as much of the dough as possible when cutting.

9. Place 1 tablespoon of filling in the middle of each circle.

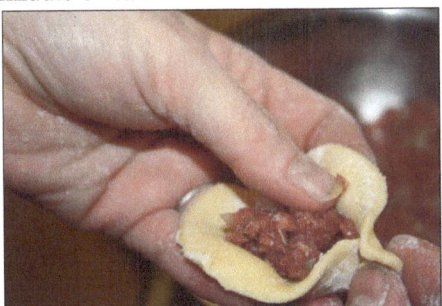

10. ▲ Next, pinch dough together to form the beginning of a half-moon shape.

11. ▲ Start to fold dough into dumpling form. Hold meat in with the left thumb, with the right hand, pinch one side in then the other.

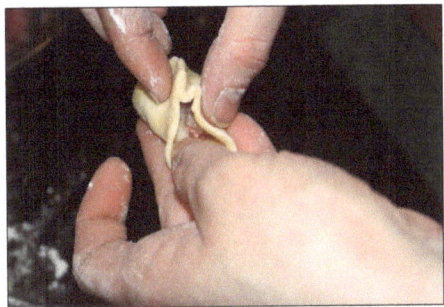

12. ▲ Continue folding in the sides of the dough.

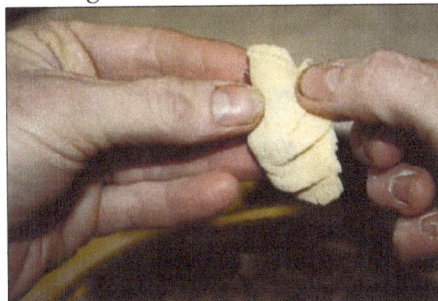

13. ▲ Side view of the dumplings while folding.

14. ▲ Fold all the way to the end.

15. ▲ Pinch the ends together. Repeat until all dough is filled and shaped.

16. Arrange dumplings in a single layer on a tray, not touching, and cover with a towel. Keep formed dumplings covered as you form them.

17. In a large pot, bring water and salt to a boil over high heat.

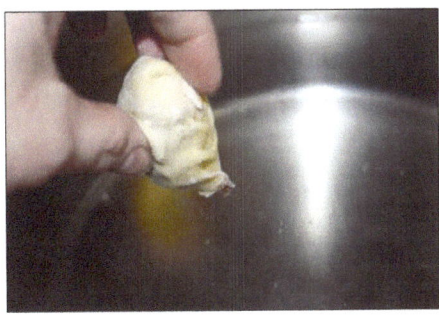

18. ▲ Add dumplings one at a time until they're all added. Cook 10 minutes or until tender.

19. ▲ The dumplings should become lighter in color and float.

Note: Test a dumpling to make sure its cooked. Bite off the tip. It should be soft. If not, continue boiling for a couple more minutes. Transfer to a serving platter when cooked. Reserve ¼ cup of broth dumplings were cooked in.

20. Prepare the first sauce: mix garlic and yogurt.

21. Prepare the second sauce: Mix vinegar, garlic and the liquid used for cooking.

22. Serve the dumplings with the two sauces in separate bowls on the side.

23. Serve warm.

Serves 8

Notes

Hajjah A'isha's Peel Meen

Hajjah Naziha grew up near the home of her maternal grandmother, Hajjah A'isha. Hajjah A'isha had embarked on a laborious two-year long *hijrah* (emigration) with her family from Kazan, Russia to Turkey, after Russia was overcome by Communism. She traveled with her four children, including Hajjah Amina ق, the mother of Hajjah Naziha. Hajjah A'isha's children ranged in age, at the time of the *hijrah*, from six months to twelve years old. After sharing this intense experience, the family's ties of religion and their familial bonds grew extremely strong.

The family settled in Damascus. Most of the extended family lived on the same property; Hajjah Naziha's grandmother, her two uncles with their wives and children and her aunt with her husband and children.

Every Thursday, His Eminence Mawlana Shaykh Nazim ق, Hajjah Amina's husband, would buy meat. On Friday, the three generations of ladies – Hajjah Naziha's grandmother A'isha, her mother Hajjah Amina ق and her aunt and her uncle's wives, and the female grandchildren, would gather to prepare the meal together. They would make the Peel Meen, a delicious Russian dish of small dumplings filled with ground beef and onions cooked together in a sumptuous tomato broth. The Peel Meen take time to form: the dough must be rolled out and filled and the dumplings, when formed, are small. After the jumu'ah prayer the family would gather to eat. All together, there were ten adults and 24 children (the grandchildren) who came. The entire family ate from the dish of Peel Meen. They had a very simple, happy life. They didn't complain.

Their grandmother A'isha would serve each of the grandchildren five or six of the Peel Meen dumplings in a bowl, along with its tomato broth. She would also give each of them a piece of bread. They would all dip the bread into tomato dumpling broth to fill their stomachs. In the end, they would eat the small dumplings so the dumpling flavor would stay with them. Hajjah A'isha carried the knowledge of this dish with her from her home country which she was forced to flee or lose her religion. Hajjah A'isha taught this dish, through the family meal on Friday, to her granddaughter, Hajjah Naziha, who always reads Surat al-Fatiha for her grandmother when preparing this dish. Hajjah Naziha's four children and ten grandchildren (as of the writing of this book!) also all love this dish. Hajjah Naziha hopes your family will enjoy it, too.

Russia
Peel-meen

Small Meat-Filled Dumplings in Savory Tomato Broth

Ingredients
Dough:
1 large egg
¾ cup water
½ teaspoon salt
3 ¼ cups flour

Filling:
¼ pound ground beef
¼ medium onion, finely chopped
¼ teaspoon salt
⅛ teaspoon black pepper

Broth:
3 tablespoons butter
½ medium onion, finely chopped
5 tablespoons tomato paste
11 cups water
4 small beef bullion cubes
2 ½ teaspoons salt

Preparation
1. To prepare dough, beat together egg, water and salt.

   Note: The egg helps keep the dough together.

2. Add flour. Knead by hand or use a mixer with a dough hook.

3. ▲ When the dough holds together and is the consistency of an earlobe, shape into a ball. Cut dough ball in half. Cover both halves with a towel or an overturned bowl, and let rest for 10-15 minutes.

4. ▲ Remove one dough ball; keeping the other one covered. Prepare a floured surface. Also lightly flour rolling pin. Start to roll out dough.

5. ▲ Continue to roll dough out by rolling around the rolling pin.
6. Roll out dough until it is 1/16-inch thick.

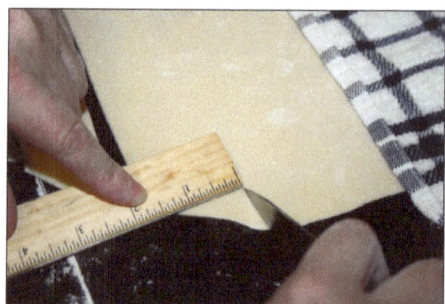

7. ▲ Once dough is rolled out, cover half with a kitchen towel. Use a ruler to

make 1 1/2 inch markings along the side of the dough.

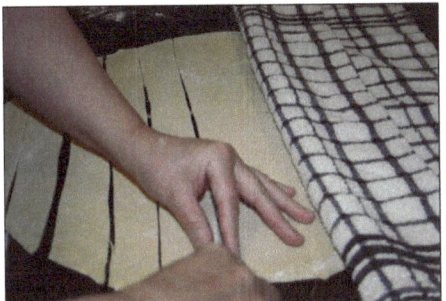

8. ▲Use a knife to cut horizontally along these markings, making 1 ½ inch thick strips of dough.

9. ▲Make markings at 1 ½ inch intervals going across the dough. Use a knife to cut along these markings.

10. ▲The dough will be cut into 1 ½ inch squares.

11. **Prepare filling:** To a bowl add: ground beef, onion, salt and pepper. Mix well.

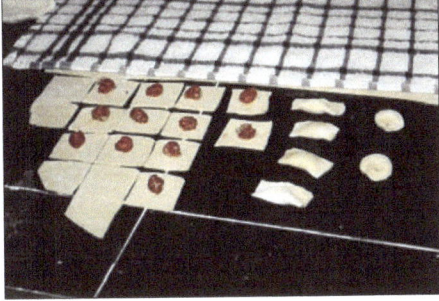

12. ▲Place ¼ teaspoon of filling in center of each square.
13. Then fold each square in half to make a rectangle with a lump of filling in the middle. Press the sides together to seal.

14. ▲Fold the small sides of the rectangle together.

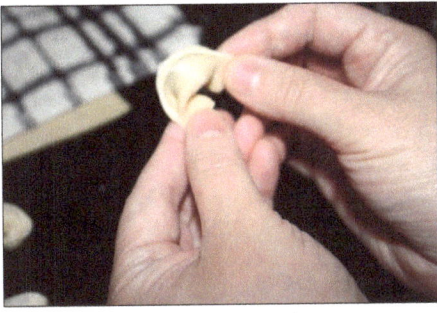

15. ▲Bring the ends together.

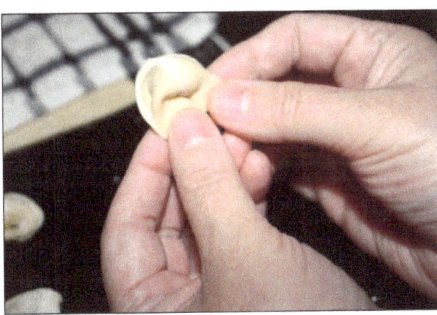

16. ▲Press corners to seal.

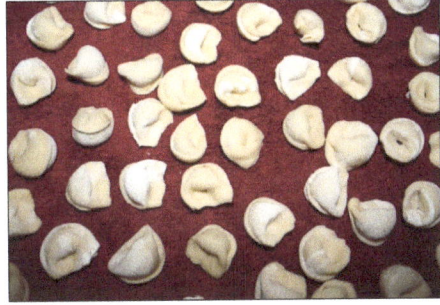

17. ▲Continue filling and sealing dough squares. Place dumplings on a tray lined with a towel. Repeat with other half of dough. Cover formed dumplings with a towel.

18. ▲**Prepare broth:** Melt butter in a soup pot on medium heat. Add onion and sauté until golden. Mix in tomato paste. Add water, chicken cubes and salt. Bring to a boil over high heat.
20. Add dumplings one at a time. Cover and return to a boil. Reduce heat to medium-low and simmer, uncovered, for 20 minutes, or until dumplings float to the top.
21. Transfer to a serving dish.

22. ▲Serve warm with yogurt, sumac and bread.

Serves 4 as a main dish.
Serves 6 as an appetizer.

Notes

Rice and Bulgur Chapter

Benefits of Rice

Hajjah Naziha relates, "The Lord created everything for some benefit for human beings. I heard from my mother, Hajjah Amina ق that He created every grain of rice with Surah Ya Sin written on it. For this reason, out of respect, we don't like to throw rice away. Try as you can to finish rice. You can turn older rice into soup."

"Rice has a healing quality; it is very good for the stomach. Traditionally, if a baby has an upset stomach, we boiled rice without washing it, and cooked it with extra water. We then gave the rice broth to the baby to stop diarrhea. We also make ground rice powdered, as the first food for babies because it is very easy for them to digest. It is good to make rice or rice soup for any sick person because it is not heavy on the stomach and also gives them energy.

"When I visited Sri Lanka, I saw, for the first time in my life, the way rice is grown. It is very different from how wheat grows. I saw people walking and bending in muddy fields. I asked, "What are they doing?" They told me the people in the fields were growing rice. *Subhan'Allah* how rice grows inside water. For the Far Eastern people rice is the staple of their diet. Whole grain rice especially has many vitamins as well as carbohydrates. In the Far East people eat just a little bit of rice and are grateful because it gives them power. Until now, many people live off of rice and lentils. Rice or bulgur and salad are staples on my table."

Mediterranean
Ruz bish-Sha`eeriyyah

Rice with Fried Noodles

A tasty alternative to plain white rice.

Ingredients
2 cups short-grain rice
3 teaspoons salt, divided
4 cups water
2 tablespoons butter
2 "nests" of birds-nest noodles or heaping 2/3 cup of Angel hair noodles (broken by hand into 1-inch pieces)
Note: The amount of noodles in a "nest" can vary considerably depending on the brand. When broken into 1-inch pieces, each "nest" should yield a heaping 1/3-cup of noodles.

Preparation
1. Rinse rice a few times until the water runs clear. Soak rice in a bowl of hot water with half a teaspoon of the salt.

2. ▲Melt butter in a pot over medium heat. When melted, add the broken noodles and sauté until golden brown, stirring constantly so they don't burn.

3. Add water and bring to a boil over high heat. Add remaining 2 ½ teaspoons of the salt to the water.
4. Drain rice and add to boiling water. Let boil for a couple of minutes, then reduce heat to medium and continue to cook, covered, for 10-15 minutes.
5. Once rice is tender, turn off heat and remove lid.
6. Place a towel over the pot and replace lid over towel. Let steam like this for 10 minutes.
7. Serve hot.

Serves 4-6

Iran
Kiase li-Pilaw

Jeweled Rice

Ingredients
4 cups basmati rice
4 ounces dried apricots; 1 cup diced
½ cup raisins
10 small chicken bullion cubes
1 cup vegetable oil
½ cup skinless, slivered almonds
½ cup pistachios
½ cup pine nuts
2 tablespoons sugar
2 large onions, finely chopped
½ teaspoon saffron in 1 tablespoon hot water
1 tablespoon salt
2 teaspoons black pepper
6 cups water

Preparation
1. Soak rice in a large bowl of hot water. Set aside for 20-30 minutes.
2. Cut apricots to 1/3 inch cubes. When cut there should be a cupful of chopped apricots.
3. Rinse raisins. Set raisins and nuts aside
4. Heat oil in a pot on high heat. When hot, add onions. Cook onions until they start to turn golden. Then add almonds, pine nuts and pistachios. Sauté nuts and onions until nuts turn golden brown.
5. Add raisins and apricots. Sauté together for 5 more minutes.
6. **Prepare chicken broth**: measure 6 cups of hot water and dissolve bullion cubes in water.
7. Drain rice. Add rice to onions, nuts and dried fruit mixture.
8. Sauté together for 5 minutes so rice absorbs flavors of other ingredients.
9. Add the salt, pepper and sugar. Mix well with the rice. Let cook for 1-2 minutes. Then pour in the chicken broth.
10. In a small bowl, mix the saffron with a tablespoon of hot water. The saffron gives a nice smell and color to the rice. There will be a few strings. They will dissolve later with cooking.
11. Pour saffron and water into rice. Mix well.
12. Bring covered pot to a boil on high heat. Let boil for 5 minutes on high heat, keeping the pot covered, stirring occasionally.
13. Reduce heat to medium. Continue cooking, covered, for 10 minutes on medium heat. Keep pot covered. Stir occasionally until rice is cooked and soft. Reduce heat to low. Continue cooking, covered, for 10 minutes.
14. When rice is cooked, turn off heat. Place a towel over the pot. Replace lid over towel. Let steam for 13 minutes, or until ready to serve. Fluff and serve.
15. Serve hot.

Serves 4-6

Lebanon
Maklube

Layered Meat, Rice and Vegetables on a Platter

Maklube is a wonderful dish. All the ingredients are placed in a pot. The pot is turned upside-down onto a platter to form a savory layered "cake" of meat, rice and vegetables for serving.

Ingredients

2 pounds boneless beef chunks

1 cup frozen peas

Preparation

▲ 4 medium potatoes, peeled and cut into ½-inch rounds
4 cups basmati rice
8 cups water (if cooking in a pressure cooker) or 14 cups water (if cooking in a pot)

▲ 1 large carrot, peeled and cut into ½-inch rounds
2 tablespoons butter
1 ½ cups vegetable oil
1 teaspoon pepper
3 teaspoons salt
1 teaspoon cinnamon
1 small onion, chopped

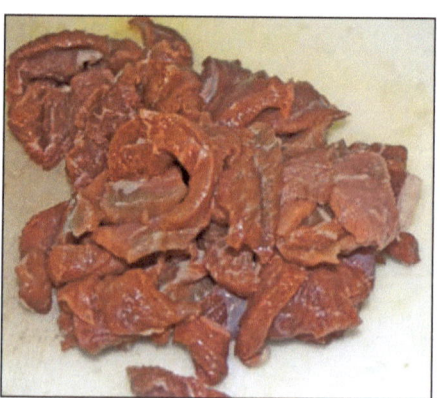

1. ▲ Cut meat into 1/8-inch slices. Rinse meat in a strainer.
2. If using a pressure cooker, place meat in with salt, pepper, cinnamon, onion and water. Bring to a boil on high heat. When pressure cooker whistles, reduce heat to low and cook for 20 minutes or until meat is tender.

3. If using a regular pot, place meat with 14 cups of water and salt, pepper, cinnamon and onion. Bring to a boil on high heat. Reduce heat to medium-low and simmer meat for an hour and 45 minutes, or until meat is tender.

Note: You can add a teaspoon of baking soda to soften the meat faster.

4. In a separate pan, heat ¾ cup of the oil on high heat. Fry potatoes until golden brown, then place on plate lined with paper towel to drain

5. ▲ In a small pan, place carrots and peas and enough water to boil. Bring to a boil on high heat. Boil for 5-10 minutes, or until cooked. Strain vegetables.

6. Open the pressure cooker or uncover the pot and remove meat with a slotted spoon, saving the broth. Place the meat, carrots, and peas in a bowl. Mix gently.

6. Rinse and soak the rice for 10 minutes in hot water. Drain rice.

7. Melt butter and ½ cup of the oil in a pan. Add boiled meat, carrots and peas. Sprinkle with salt and pepper. Sauté together for about 5 minutes or until the meat begins to brown.

8. ▲ In a soup pot or large wide pot, start to layer ingredients. First place a layer of cooked potatoes in bottom of pot. Place meat and vegetables over potatoes.

9. ▲ Pour rice over meat and vegetables. Level rice with the back of a spoon (to have an even layer).

10. ▲ Then, very slowly, gently pour over the rice 6 cups of meat broth. Cover and reduce heat to medium-low. Cook for approximately 20 minutes or until rice is cooked.

11. Once rice is cooked, turn off heat and remove lid. Place a towel over the pot and replace lid over towel. Let steam like this for 5-10 minutes. Remove from stove and let cool for 15 minutes.

12. Remove lid. Place a large serving plate over the top of the pan and gently flip the pan over. Slowly lift the pot straight up so the layers remain as intact as possible; like a savory layered cake with potatoes on top and rice on bottom.

13. Serve hot.

Serves 6-8

Cyprus
Domatesli Pirinç Pilavı

Tomato Rice

Ingredients
3 cups short-grain rice
2 tablespoons butter
1 small onion, finely chopped
3 medium tomatoes
4 ½ cups water
2 teaspoons salt, divided
2 tablespoons tomato paste

Preparation
1. Rinse rice a few times, until the water runs clear. Soak rice in a bowl of hot water with a teaspoon of salt, between 20-30 minutes.
2. In a large pot, melt butter on medium-high heat. Add onions and sauté until golden brown, stirring constantly.
3. Grate tomatoes. Discard peel. Mix into onion.
4. Cover pan and cook tomatoes and onions on low heat for 5-10 minutes or until tomatoes are very soft. Mix in tomato paste.
5. Add water to pot and bring to a boil on high heat. Add remaining 1 teaspoon of the salt to the water.
6. Strain rice. Add rice to boiling water and cover. Bring to a boil stirring once. After 3 minutes reduce heat to medium low. Let simmer, covered, till water is absorbed, between 5-10 minutes. Once the liquid is absorbed and small craters form, stir once more.
7. Reduce heat to low. Cook, still covered, for 5 minutes or until rice is done.

Note: Taste a little bit of rice to make sure it is done. Different rice has different cook times.

8. Turn off heat, but keep pot on stove. Cover pot with a towel. Replace lid over towel. Let steam like this for 5 minutes.
9. Serve hot.

Serves 4-6

Turkey
Domatesli Bulgur Pilavi

Bulgur and Onions

Bulgur (a form of cracked wheat), prepared with sautéed tomatoes and onions, is a flavorful alternative to rice.

Ingredients
3 cups bulgur
1 large onion, finely chopped
4 tablespoons butter
½ cup vegetable oil
2 tomatoes
2 tablespoons tomato paste
2 chicken bullion cubes (optional)
2 teaspoons salt
4 cups water

Preparation
1. Wash and drain bulgur.
2. Grate tomatoes and discard skin.
3. In a soup pot, heat oil and butter. Once butter is melted, add chopped onions and sauté until onions are soft and transparent. Add grated tomatoes and cook for about two minutes

4. ▲ Dissolve tomato paste in half a cup of water and stir into onions and tomatoes. Mix well.
5. In the four cups of water, put the bullion cubes and salt to dissolve. Once dissolved, add to the tomatoes. Cover and bring to a boil on high heat.

6. ▲ When water boils, add bulgur. Mix so that bulgur is level in the pan.

7. ▲ To test to see if there is enough bulgur, put a wooden spoon in different places in the pot. If the spoon stands up by itself, the bulgur is right. If the spoon falls, you need to add a little more bulgur.
8. Reduce the heat to medium and cook, covered, for 15 minutes. Then turn off the heat, but keep the pot on the stove.

9. ▲ Cover pot with a towel. Replace lid over the towel and let steam like this for 5 minutes.
10. Fluff and serve.
11. Serve hot. Serve with yogurt and cucumber salad.
Serves 6-8

Lebanon
Riz bil Foul al-Akhdar

Green Fava Bean Pilau with Beef Chunks

Ingredients
1 pound boneless beef chunks, cut into 1-inch cubes
1 pound green fava beans (available seasonally at Middle Eastern stores)
½ cup butter
2 large onions, chopped
5 cups water
1 ½ cups short-grain rice
1 teaspoon salt
1 teaspoon pepper
1 teaspoon cinnamon

Preparation

1. ▲ **Shell fava beans:** Open pods and remove beans. Rinse shelled beans.

2. ▲ To a non-stick medium-sized pot add meat. Sauté meat until juice is released and goes back in, stirring occasionally over high heat. Add butter and onions. Saute together until onions become transparent and the meat is golden brown. Add salt, pepper, and cinnamon.
3. Add water. Cover with the lid. Bring to a boil. Reduce heat to medium, and boil for 45 minutes, or until meat is tender.

4. ▲ Add fava beans to pot. Cover and return to a boil on high heat. Let boil for 15 minutes.
5. Rinse rice. Add rice to pot. Cook, covered, on low heat for 20 minutes, or until rice is cooked and all of the broth has been absorbed.
6. Once rice is tender, turn off heat and remove lid. Place a towel over the pot and replace lid over towel. Let steam like this for 10 minutes.
7. Serve hot.

Serves 2-4

Poultry Chapter

Cypriot Chickens

Hajjah Naziha relates, "My father, Mawlana Shaykh Nazim ق, never liked to eat chickens from the market. For this reason, my mother, Hajjah Amina ق used to raise chicks to have homegrown eggs and chickens. She kept chickens and at least one rooster for producing eggs in our yard."

"My mother would raise 20-25 small chicks at a time. She'd feed them ground barley and old bread soaked in water. She would cut cucumbers, parsley, and zucchini very small to feed them. She also gave them special vitamins to grow strong and healthy. This chicken meat was a much darker brown than the chicken you buy in the market."

"I remember one batch of the chicks was very different. Twenty of the chicks became roosters and only five became hens. When my father sneezed, the leader chick would become scared of the sneezing sound and make a special 'alarm' noise. This alarm would make all of the other chicks freeze and become quiet. Then the leader chick would make another noise signaling, 'Danger Over' and then the chicks would all start talking, moving, and eating again. Every morning my family was awakened at Fajr by at least 10 roosters."

"Our favorite chicken dish was 'Makarnalı Bulli' (Crispy Chicken Over Cheesy Tubular Pasta in this chapter)."

Till now, His Eminence Mawlana Shaykh Nazim ق has lots of chickens and chicks in his yard. Amazingly, the cats at his home have never eaten the chicks and chickens. He still prefers to eat only homegrown chickens and eggs. His daughter, Hajjah Naziha, continues this practice at her own home. The chickens from her coop produce around 200 eggs every day, which are used to feed the many guests that pass through her blessed home.

Asia

Chicken with Bell Peppers

Ingredients

2 ¼ pounds chicken breasts (2 pairs)
2 tablespoons sesame oil
1 small fresh jalapeno pepper

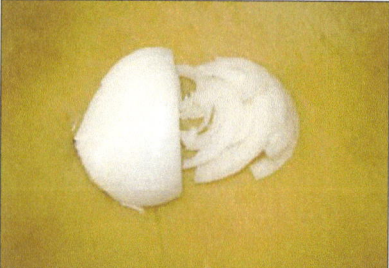

▲ 3 thinly sliced medium onions

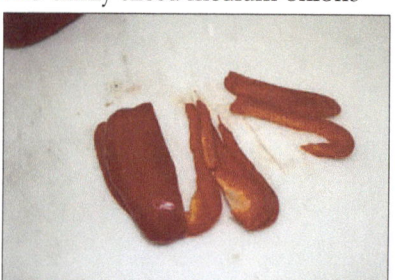

▲ 6 bell peppers; deseeded, stems removed and thinly sliced to ¼-inch strips. Use 2 green, 2 red, 2 yellow.
2 packets fajita seasoning
1 cup water
2 cups minced cilantro

Preparation

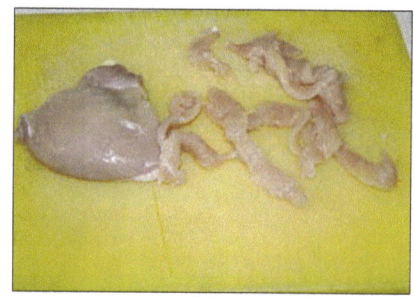

1. ▲ Cut the chicken breasts into ¼-inch thick strips.

2. ▲ In a wok or large pot, heat the two oils. When hot, add the chicken and stir-fry until golden-brown
3. Mix in onions and cook until limp, but still white. Mix in peppers. Cover and cook for 15 minutes, stirring occasionally.
4. Dissolve fajita packet seasoning in the water in a small bowl. Mix into the chicken and peppers.
5. Reduce the heat to low. Cover and cook for 15 minutes (depending on how "done" you like the peppers). Stir in cilantro. Turn off the heat.
6. Serve hot, with fajitas, rice or pita bread.

Serves 4

Turkey
Beşamelli Karnıbahar

Chicken and Cauliflower with Béchamel Sauce

Ingredients

half a chicken
1 whole onion
2 tablespoons + 1 teaspoon salt, divided
2 teaspoons white pepper, divided
3 pounds cauliflower florets
3 carrots, sliced into rounds
2 cups sweet peas
3 tablespoons butter, divided

Béchamel Sauce

4 cups milk
3 eggs
2 teaspoons salt
½ cup flour
4 tablespoons butter

Preparation

1. Place chicken in a soup pot with whole onion, 2 tablespoons of the salt and a teaspoon of the pepper. Bring to a boil over high heat. Reduce heat to medium and cook for 45 minutes, or until chicken is tender. Remove to cool.
2. Remove chicken skin and cut meat into small pieces. Set aside.
3. Boil cauliflower florets until firm but cooked. Drain in a strainer and rinse with cold water.
4. Sauté carrots in 2 tablespoons of the butter for about 5 minutes or until carrots are softened. Add peas and sauté together for another 10 minutes. Add a teaspoon each of the salt and the pepper.

5. ▲ Add chicken pieces. Mix well.
6. Grease a baking dish with butter. Put ½ of the cauliflower in the bottom of the baking dish. Then sprinkle chicken and vegetable mixture over cauliflower, covering the bottom layer.

7. ▲ Add the rest of the cauliflower on top of the chicken and vegetable mixture, to cover.

8. **Prepare the béchamel sauce:** mix milk, eggs, salt and flour together in a mixing bowl. Melt the butter in a pan. Then pour the milk mixture into the pan. Stir constantly, using a whisk. Once it starts to thicken, remove from heat.

9. ▲ Pour over the top of the cauliflower

Note: If you cook the béchamel sauce too long it will be too thick and will have lumps.

10. Bake at 350°F for 40 minutes, or until the top turns a golden color.

Serves 6-8

Iran
Morgheh Tu Pour Ba Esfenaj Wa Paneer

Stuffed Chicken Breasts

Ingredients
1 pound chopped frozen spinach
2 pounds chicken breasts (2 pairs)
7 tablespoons butter, divided
½ cup pine nuts
6 cloves crushed garlic
1 teaspoon salt
½ teaspoon white pepper
1 packet phyllo dough (available in freezer section of grocery store)
½ cup grated parmesan cheese

Note: Use phyllo dough that is at room temperature. Cover with a towel as soon as the package is opened to prevent the phyllo from drying out.

Preparation
1. Preheat oven to 375°F
2. Take out spinach to thaw.

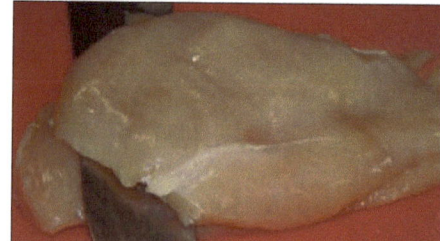

3. ▲ Cut each chicken breast through the middle so it's half as thick. Lay flat on the counter, position knife in the middle and slice through. You should have 8 pieces of chicken breast after cutting all the chicken.
4. Remove fat from chicken. Place each chicken breast between two pieces of plastic wrap so it doesn't splatter when tenderizing.

5. ▲ Tenderize each cut breast with smooth side of meat mallet until ½ centimeter thick. If breast becomes very big when tenderizing, than cut in half.
6. Melt 3 tablespoons of the butter in a saucepan over medium heat. When melted, add garlic and sauté until golden brown. Mix the salt and pepper into the garlic. Set aside.

7. n a separate saucepan, melt 2 tablespoons of the butter over medium heat. Add pine nuts and sauté until golden brown. Immediately remove from heat and set aside.

8. Squeeze water from thawing spinach. Mix butter and garlic mixture into spinach.

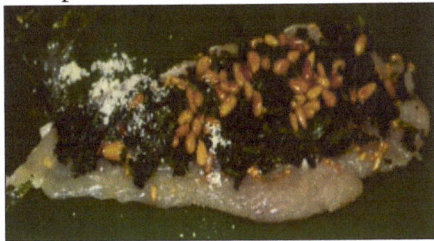

9. ▲Lay the chicken breast flat. Spread 2 tablespoons of spinach mixture evenly over breast. Sprinkle about a tablespoon of pine nuts over spinach. Sprinkle evenly 3 tablespoons of parmesan cheese over spinach and pinenuts.

10. Start rolling breast up at the widest end. Roll up the chicken breast, keeping the filling inside. Set aside.

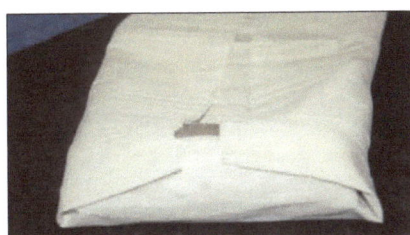

11. ▲Take 2 sheets of phyllo dough. Place the chicken about two inches from the edge of the phyllo dough. Fold the end of the dough over the chicken. Fold the sides over the chicken.

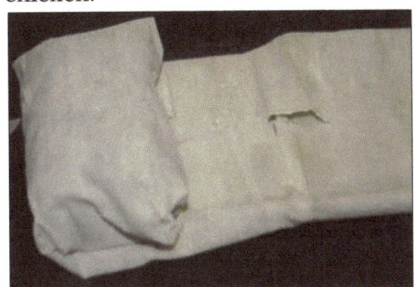

12. ▲Start to roll the filled chicken breast up in the phyllo dough.

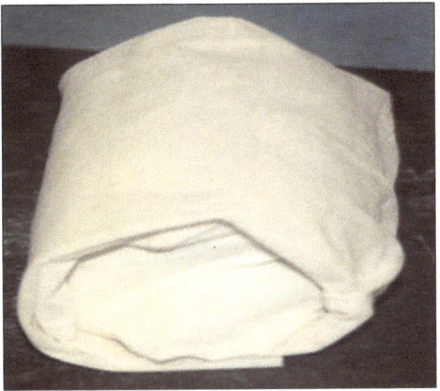

13. ▲Roll all the way to the end, like an egg roll. Place open end down on cookie sheet. Continue with the same method for the remaining chicken breasts and phyllo dough. Place finished rolls on cookie sheet as they are done.

14. Melt the remaining two tablespoons of butter. Spoon about one teaspoon of the melted butter over each roll. Makes about 8 rolls

15. Bake at 375°F for 50 minutes, or until golden brown on top.

16. Arrange rolls on a serving platter. Serve warm.

Serves 8

Lebanon
Dajaaj wa Jazr bis-Salsatal-Bayda

Chicken with Carrots in White Sauce

Ingredients
12 chicken drumsticks
1 lemon, cut in half
½ cup vegetable oil
1½ tablespoons butter
1 pound carrots (about 5 large), peeled and cut into ¼-inch rounds
1 teaspoon salt
¼ teaspoon white pepper

Sauce
2 tablespoons butter
½ cup flour
3 cups milk
½ teaspoon white pepper
1 teaspoon salt

Preparation
1. Preheat oven to 400°F.
2. Rub chicken with lemon halves (the lemon removes the chicken smell). Discard lemon. Rinse chicken
3. Put chicken pieces in a baking pan. Sprinkle with salt and pepper.

4. ▲ Bake uncovered on middle rack for 50 minutes, or until golden brown.
5. Melt 1½ tablespoons of butter on medium heat in a small saucepan.

6. ▲ Add carrots and sauté in butter for ten minutes or until soft but not at all darkened. Be careful not to let the carrots get brown, as that will affect the taste of the sauce.
7. **Prepare the sauce**: melt butter over medium heat. Add flour.
8. Whisk in milk, white pepper, and salt. Whisk until sauce starts to thicken.

9. ▲ Mix carrots into the sauce.
Note: Do *not* make the sauce until you're ready to serve.
10. Pour the sauce and carrots over the chicken. Broil at 500°F on the middle rack of the oven for 5-7 minutes or until lightly brown on top.
11. Serve hot.

Serves 4-6

Lebanon
Dajaaj Mishwee

Roasted Chicken

Ingredients
1 chicken
1 tablespoon lemon juice or 1 quartered fresh lemon
1 teaspoon salt
1 teaspoon pepper
1 teaspoon cinnamon

Preparation
1. Preheat oven to 400°F.
2. Rinse chicken. Rub chicken with lemon juice, or cut lemon (lemon reduces smell of the chicken).
3. Rinse chicken again and sprinkle with salt, pepper and cinnamon on all sides. Rub seasoning into chicken.
4. Bake covered for 1 ½ hours. Uncover and bake for 15-20 minutes to brown.
5. Serve hot.

Note: Also tasty when cooked in a rotisserie oven. Add 1 teaspoon of coriander to cavity of chicken. Don't truss. Cook for 1 hour and 15 minutes.

Serve 2-4

Lebanon
Dajaaj ma` Fatr wa Bandurah

Chicken with Mushrooms and Tomatoes

Ingredients
1 chicken, cut into 8 pieces
½ cup vegetable oil
½ cup olive oil
3 garlic cloves, cut into rounds
4 tablespoons butter
1 8-ounces package fresh mushrooms, sliced
1 large bell pepper, cut into ½-inch cubes
2 teaspoons salt
1 teaspoon pepper
2 teaspoons rosemary
½ teaspoon cinnamon
4 large tomatoes, peeled and cut into chunks
4 tablespoons tomato paste
½ cup chopped parsley
1½ cups water

Preparation
1. Preheat oven to 400°F.
2. Rinse chicken. Remove skin and fat.

3. ▲ Heat both oils over high heat. When hot, add garlic. Cooking the garlic gives the oil a nice flavor.

4. ▲ Add chicken. Reduce heat to medium. Fry until chicken is golden brown on both sides.
5. Drain chicken for 10 minutes in a colander to remove excess oil. The garlic will become black; discard garlic when chicken is done.
6. Place chicken in baking dish.

7. ▲ In a separate pan, melt butter over medium heat. Add mushrooms.
8. Mix peppers into the mushrooms. Saute for 5 minutes.
9. Mix in salt, pepper, rosemary, cinnamon, chopped tomatoes, and tomato paste. Cook together for 5 minutes. Pour over chicken.
10. Sprinkle with parsley. Pour in water from a corner of the dish.
11. Cover and bake for one hour.
12. Serve hot with rice.

Serves 4-6

Cyprus
Makarnah Bulli

Crispy Chicken Over Cheesy Tubular Pasta

Ingredients
1 whole chicken with skin
1 tablespoon salt
½ teaspoon white pepper
1 small whole onion
1 cup corn oil for frying chicken
   (no oil needed for broiler version)
1 pound macaroni pastitsio
   (Middle Eastern store) or bucatini
   pasta (grocery store)
8 ounces or 2 ¼ cups grated Haloum
   or Mozzarella cheese
1 tablespoon dried mint

Preparation

1. ▲ Put whole chicken in a soup pot, with water to cover, salt, white pepper and a whole onion.
2. Cover and bring to a boil on high heat. Remove lid and skim the foam from the top. Reduce heat to medium-high and boil, partially covered, for 45 minutes or until chicken is tender. Meanwhile skim any other foam that forms as it simmers.
   Note: Check to see if chicken is done by poking breast with a fork. If the water that comes out is clear, then it is cooked. If not, continue boiling until done.
3. Remove chicken from broth and place in a strainer to drain excess water. Reserve broth in pot.
4. Either fry or broil the whole chicken. The traditional Cypriot method is to fry. To broil go to **Step 7**.
5. **To fry**: Warm oil over high heat. When hot, add chicken and fry until dark golden brown on bottom.

6. ▲ Turn over and brown other side. Brown the sides by holding chicken up with a spatula on its sides. Try not to turn chicken too many times or it will fall apart while cooking. Go to **Step 8**.
7. **To broil**: Place whole chicken under broiler in a pan on middle rack of a preheated oven. Broil for 15 minutes on first side; then flip and broil for 15 minutes on other side until golden brown.
8. Break pasta into 1-inch pieces.
9. Mix grated cheese and mint in a bowl.
10. Remove onion from broth. Bring chicken broth to boil over high heat.
11. Add pasta and boil until tender, according to package directions.
12. Remove pasta with a slotted spoon and place on serving plate.

13. ▲ Sprinkle Haloum cheese and mint over pasta. The heat from the noodles will melt the cheese a little.
14. Break chicken into pieces and place on top of cheese.
15. Serve hot.

Serves 2-4

Lebanon
Dajaaj Mahshee

Stuffed Chicken with Savory Rice and Ground Beef

This is a special Lebanese recipe for a tasty, dark golden stuffed chicken served surrounded by a savory, meat and pine nut-filled rice. The recipe was traditionally prepared by Hajjah Yousra by stuffing the chicken, then frying it, and finally boiling it. The broth made from boiling the chicken is used to prepare a spectacular rice which is served with it. A baking variation is given at the end of the recipe for a time-saving option.

Ingredients
1 whole chicken
1 tablespoon lemon juice or 1 quartered fresh lemon
1 teaspoon salt
½ teaspoon pepper
½ teaspoon cinnamon
3 cups oil (for frying)
10 cups water

Filling
¼ pound ground beef
½ teaspoon salt
¼ teaspoon pepper
¼ teaspoon cinnamon
1 tablespoon butter
3 tablespoons pine nuts

3 tablespoons rice, preferably short-grain
1 cup water

Preparation
1. Rinse chicken. Rub chicken with lemon juice, or cut lemon (lemon reduces smell of the chicken). Rinse again.
2. Sprinkle chicken evenly with salt, pepper, and cinnamon. Place in a baking pan.
3. **Prepare stuffing**: in a separate pan, cook the ground beef, salt, pepper and cinnamon over medium-high meat. Cook meat until dark brown.
4. In a small saucepan, melt butter. Add pine nuts and sauté until golden. Add pine nuts and butter to ground beef. Mix well.

5. ▲ Stir the rice and water into the ground beef mixture.

6. ▲ Cook, partially uncovered, on medium-low heat, until rice is tender. Stir occasionally.

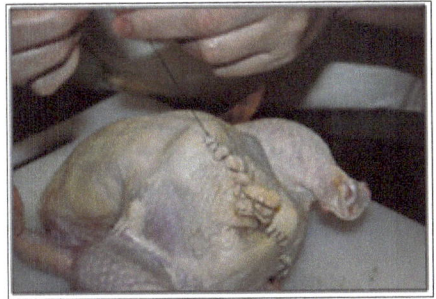

9. ▲ Sew cavity completely closed.

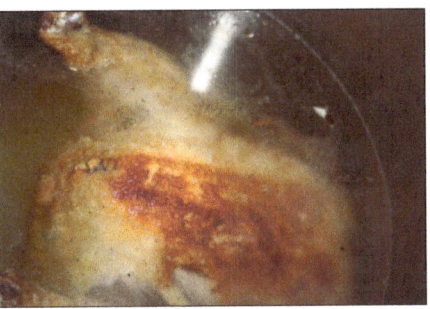

12. ▲ Once the water is boiling, place browned chicken and cook for 40 minutes, or until chicken is cooked.
13. Carefully lift chicken from water. Reserve chicken broth to prepare the rice below.
14. Place chicken on a plate.
15. Serve hot.

Baked variation: Preheat oven to 350° F. After Step 9, cover stuffed chicken with foil and bake for 1 ½ hours. Remove foil and cook uncovered for 10 to 15 minutes, or until chicken is a deep golden brown.

Serves 4-6

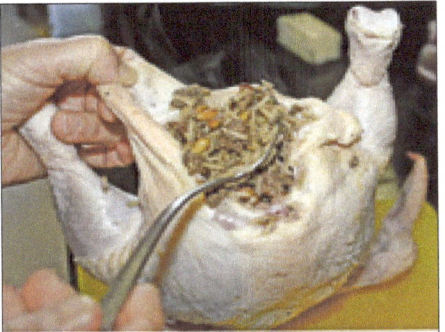

7. ▲ Spoon stuffing into chicken cavity.

10. ▲ **Fry stuffed chicken:** Heat oil in a large wok or pan on high heat. When oil is hot, carefully place chicken in oil, breast-side down. Fry until chicken is a dark golden brown. Then, using your hand and a spatula, carefully turn chicken over to brown the back side of the chicken. Once the chicken is a dark golden brown remove from the oil.
11. Meanwhile, in a soup pot, bring water to a boil on high heat.

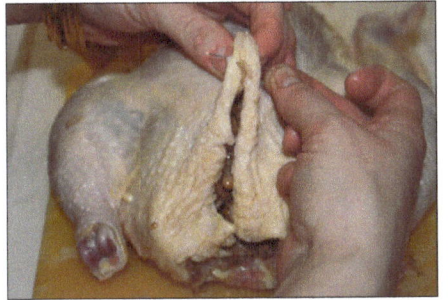

8. ▲ Sew the cavity closed using a dark string. Start at the top of the cavity.

Meat and Nut-Filled Rice to Accompany Stuffed Chicken

Ingredients
3 cups rice, preferably short-grain
¾ pound ground beef
1 small onion, finely chopped
2 teaspoons salt
1 teaspoon pepper
1 teaspoon cinnamon
½ cup pine nuts
3 tablespoons butter
5 cups chicken broth (from above recipe or using 4 small bullion cubes dissolved in water).

Preparation:
1. Brown ground beef and onions over medium-high heat in a large pot. Mix in salt, pepper and cinnamon.
2. Melt 1 tablespoon of butter in a small saucepan. Add pine nuts and sauté until golden-brown. Add pine nuts and any pan drippings to the meat. Set aside.
3. Wash and drain rice. Pour chicken broth into ground beef mixture. Bring to a boil on high heat.
4. Add rice. Let boil for a couple of minutes, then reduce heat to medium and continue to cook, covered, for 10-15 minutes.
5. Once rice is tender, turn off heat and remove lid. Place a towel over the pot and replace lid over towel. Let steam like this for 10 minutes.
6. Place around chicken on platter.
7. Serve hot.

Serves 4-6

Fish and Seafood Chapter

Importance of Fish

Hajjah Nazihe states: "Our Lord created everything for a reason. He created fish for the benefit of humanity. Fish is nutritious, very easy to digest, and has traditionally been known to improve memory."

Coastal cities and towns have always been blessed to get fresh fish. However, it was also important for people who lived inland to have fish. Thus, inland towns used to get their fish preserved in salt. All fish can be preserved and transported in salt, but sardines are most often preserved because their bones dissolve in the salt. Merchants would pack the fish and transport it on the backs of donkeys and camels to special fish markets. Whole fish were packed in wooden boxes. The bottom layer of the box was rock salt (that does not dissolve quickly), the second layer was fish, and the third layer was rock salt, and so on until the entire box was filled. The first and last layers were always salt. The fish was not scaled before it was packed. When it arrived at the market, people would buy it, take it home, and clean it.

To clean the fish, they put a little vinegar in a plate, and dipped both sides of the fish in it. They then lightly descaled the fish with a knife. The salt-packed fish cooked by itself within the three weeks it took to transport it to inland markets. No further cooking was necessary, once cleaned it was served as a meal with bread or as a side dish for flavor.

Fish is still eaten like this in Turkey and Cyprus, where it is known as *sardalli*, and in Egypt, where it known as *faseekh*. Today fresh fish can be transported in airplanes therefore salted fish is now served as a part of the region's rich cultural history rather than out of necessity.

Fish Preparation Instructions

The following is the way to clean and marinate fish for many of the recipes in this chapter. Below is the proportion for cleaning and marinating one fish. Double or triple, depending on the recipe.

Ingredients
1 whole fish with skin, 1 ½ -2 pounds
1 lemon or ½ lemon and ½ lime, thinly sliced
1 medium onion, thinly sliced
1 teaspoon salt

Preparation
1. Clean fish for immediate use or if freezing for later use: remove gills (if not done already) and open the stomach. When you open the fish there will be a dark black substance, slightly gelatinous, which is the leftover blood from the fish. Remove all of this. It is this black substance that makes the fish smell very bad when cooking.

Note: Hajjah Naziha recommends cleaning the fish with a tiny bit of soap, and then rinsing very well to remove the soap before cooking.

2. Mix lemons and onions in a large bowl.
3. Rub the inside of the fish with 1 teaspoon of the salt.

4. ▲ Stuff each fish with a handful of lemon and onion mixture.

5. ▲ Put some lemon and onion mixture under stuffed fish.

6. ▲ Sprinkle remaining lemon onion mixture over fish. Cover bowl with plastic wrap. Let marinate for at least 1 hour.
Use as needed.

Lebanon
Sayyidiah

Fisherman's Rice

Ingredients
1 black snapper fish, 1 ½ -2 pounds
1 ½ cups corn oil for frying

Rice
3 cups rice
2 teaspoons salt
4 medium onions, chopped
1 tablespoon + 1 teaspoon cumin
5 cups water

Garnish
4 tablespoons butter, divided
½ cup pine nuts
½ cup almonds

Preparation:
1. **Prepare fish:** Follow **Fish Preparation Instructions** at beginnning of chapter.
2. Remove lemons and onions from fish.

3. ▲ Heat the oil in a large skillet for frying on high heat. Sprinkle ½ teaspoon of salt into oil so it won't splatter. When oil is hot, add fish, and fry for 5-7 minutes on each side, until a dark golden brown.

4. **Debone fish:** Using your fingers, pick the fish off of the bone. The fish will come off in flaky, bite-sized pieces. Also remove any skin and discard.
5. Take a half cup of the oil used for frying fish.
6. Rinse rice. Soak rice in a large bowl with 1 teaspoon of salt and plenty of hot water to cover. Set aside.
7. In a large pot re-heat the oil used for frying the fish on high heat. When the oil is hot, add the chopped onions. Cook, stirring constantly, until the onions are a very dark brown but not burned.
8. Add 5 cups of water to the onions. Take the pot off of the heat, and move back so that the steam formed when adding the water does not burn you. Add the cumin and remaining one tablespoon of salt to the water.

9. ▲ Put a strainer over a bowl and when the water boils, use a slotted spoon to remove the onion pieces. Then press the onions with a spoon to squeeze out any excess juice. It is the taste of the dark brown onions along with the cumin that gives the Sayyidiah rice its distinctive flavor.
10. Put the strained water back in the pot. Return to a boil on high heat. Drain the rice and add to the pot. Cook, covered, for 15-20 minutes over medium heat, or until the rice is cooked and there is no more water.
11. Melt 2 tablespoons of butter in a small saucepan on medium heat. Add the pine nuts and sauté until golden brown. Place in a bowl to cool.
12. Melt remaining 2 tablespoons of butter in a small saucepan. Add almonds and sauté until golden brown. Transfer to bowl with pine nuts. Set aside.
13. Fluff rice and place on serving platter. Sprinkle de-boned fish evenly pine nuts and almonds over rice.
14. Serve hot with **Garlic and Lemon Dipping Sauce** or **Tahini Dipping Sauce**; see recipes at end of chapter.

Serves 4-6

America

Baked Salmon with Garlic

Ingredients
1 head chopped garlic
1 tablespoon chopped ginger
½ cup lemon juice
½ cup olive oil
2 teaspoons salt
½ teaspoon pepper
1 teaspoon paprika
2 teaspoons cumin powder
1 tablespoon crushed pepper flakes or chopped fresh chili pepper (optional)
1 ½ pounds salmon fish steak (1 large fish steak)

Garnish
lemon pieces and parsley

Preparation
1. **Prepare marinade:** in a bowl mix garlic, ginger, lemon juice, olive oil, and all spices.
2. Preheat oven to 450°F.

3. ▲ Place salmon in a Ziploc bag. Pour marinade over the salmon and let marinate for at least 1 hour.

4. ▲ Place salmon on a baking sheet with the skin-side down. Pour some of marinade over the salmon to form a nice garlic crust.
5. Bake for 1 hour, or until salmon is golden brown; don't flip the salmon during cooking.
6. Remove salmon using 2 metal spatulas (so it doesn't crumble easily).

Note: Plastic spatulas usually break the salmon because their edges aren't as sharp when they go underneath the fish. Place one spatula at each end and slowly lift on to the serving plate.

7. Place lemon pieces and parsley around the salmon to garnish.
8. Serve hot.

Serves 2-4.

Lebanon
Samka Harrah

Spicy Fried Fish

A tasty dish which can be prepared using leftover fish (start at Step 6 in Preparation if using leftover fish).

Ingredients
2 black snapper fish, 1 ½ – 2 pounds each
2 cups vegetable oil

For Mixture
½ cup fish oil (from frying)
4 tablespoons chopped garlic
3 bunches cilantro, finely chopped
½ cup lemon juice
1 tablespoon minced jalapeno pepper
1 teaspoon paprika
1 teaspoon salt
2 teaspoons cumin

Preparation:
1. **Prepare fish:** Follow **Fish Preparation Instructions** at beginnning of chapter. Remove lemon pieces.

2. ▲ Heat oil for frying in a large skillet on high heat. Put a ½ teaspoon of salt into the oil so it won't splatter. When the oil is hot, add fish, and fry each one for about 5-7 minutes on each side, until a dark golden brown. Remove from oil and set aside to cool.

3. ▲ **Debone fish:** pick fish off of bones. Fish will come off in flaky, bite-sized pieces. Remove any skin from fish. Discard bones and skin.
Reserve fish head and tail for serving (optional).
4. Heat ½ cup of oil on high heat. When hot, add the garlic.

5. ▲ When garlic is golden, add cilantro.
6. When the cilantro becomes soft, stir in the fish pieces, lemon juice, jalapeno pepper, paprika, salt, and cumin. Mix well. Cook together for 5 minutes. Place on a serving platter with fish head and tail.
7. Serve at room temperature with lemon juice and pita bread.
Serves 2-4.

Lebanon
Samak Mishwee bil-Farn

Baked Snapper

Ingredients
2 black snapper fish, 1 ½ -2 pounds each

Filling
2 ½ tablespoons chopped garlic
½ cup olive oil
1 teaspoon salt
2 teaspoons cumin

Preparation
1. **Prepare fish**: Follow **Fish Preparation Instructions** at beginnning of chapter.
2. Preheat oven to 450°F.
3. Remove onion and lemon from the fish.
4. **Prepare filling:** in a bowl combine garlic, olive oil, salt, and cumin. Mix well and set aside.
5. Lay the fish out on a large piece of aluminum foil.

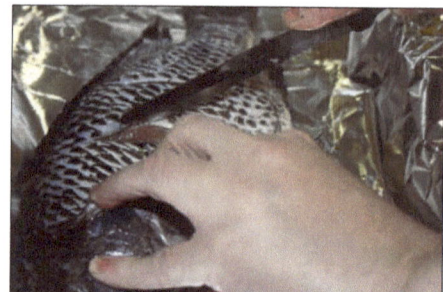

6. ▲Make 2 deep slits on both sides of the fish.

7. ▲Pack the filling in each of the slits and inside the fish. Also rub some of the filling on the outside of the fish.

8. ▲Wrap the fish in the aluminum foil piece.

   Note: Before wrapping, spread a tablespoon of olive oil on the aluminum foil so it won't stick.

9. Place in the preheated oven and bake for one hour, or until fish is tender. Open aluminum foil, exposing top of fish. Broil on middle rack in oven for 2-5 minutes, until fish is slightly crispy.

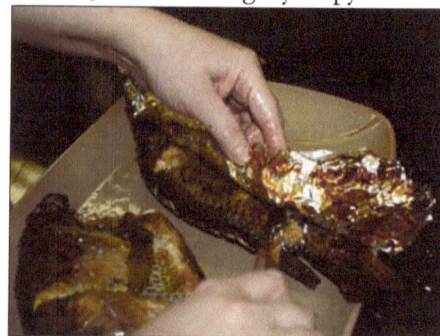

10. ▲Carefully remove fish from aluminum foil; using a fork to gently pry it off. Some fish skin may still stick to the aluminum foil. Oftentimes this fish is served inside the aluminum foil it was cooked in; just remove the extra foil around it. Place fish on a serving platter.
11. Serve hot with **Garlic and Lemon Dipping Sauce** or **Tahini Dipping Sauce**; see recipes at end of chapter.

Serves 2-4

Mediterranean
Semak Sultaan Ibraheem

Sultan Ibraheem Fish

Ingredients
6 red mullet fish or "Sultan Ibraheem" fish
flour (to dredge)
2 cups oil (for frying)

Preparation
1. **Prepare fish:** Follow **Fish Preparation Instructions** at beginnning of chapter. As the red mullet fish are relatively small, you just need half the onions and lemons to marinate them.
2. Remove the lemons and onions.

3. ▲ Sprinkle a plate liberally with flour. Dredge fish in the flour.
4. Heat oil for frying on high heat.
5. Shake excess flour off of fish onto plate.

6. ▲ When oil is hot, fry fish. Fry for 3 minutes on each side, until crispy and golden brown.
7. Serve hot with **Garlic and Lemon Dipping Sauce**; see recipe at end of chapter.

Serves 2-4

Lebanon
Qareedis Mishwee

Grilled Shrimp

Mawlana Shaykh Hisham's mother, Hajjah Yousra, often prepared this shrimp dish for her family.

Ingredients
24 ounces colossal shrimp
1 head chopped garlic
1 tablespoon chopped ginger
2 teaspoons salt
1 teaspoon pepper
½ teaspoon paprika
½ teaspoon dried basil
½ cup lemon juice
½ cup olive oil

Garnish
Lemon pieces and parsley

Preparation
1. **Devein the shrimp** (if necessary): remove shrimp veins with your fingers or a small knife. Rinse shrimp in a strainer and leave to drain.
2. **Prepare marinade:** in a bowl combine garlic, ginger, salt, pepper, paprika, basil, lemon juice, and olive oil. Mix well.
3. Place shrimp in a Ziploc bag. Pour marinade into bag, seal and mix shrimp in. Let marinate for at least 1 hour.
4. Grill shrimp on either a barbeque or electric grill. Grill for approximately 3 ½ minutes on each side.
5. Transfer to a serving plate. Garnish with lemon pieces and parsley.
6. Serve hot.

Serves 4

Turkey
Hindistancevizli Karides

Coconut Shrimp

Ingredients
4 pounds colossal shrimp
4 eggs
1 ½ teaspoons salt
3 cups shredded coconut
1 cup flour
2 cups oil (for frying)

Preparation
1. Wash the shrimp. Leave tail on.
2. **Devein shrimp:** remove shrimp veins with your fingers or a small knife. Rinse shrimp in a strainer.

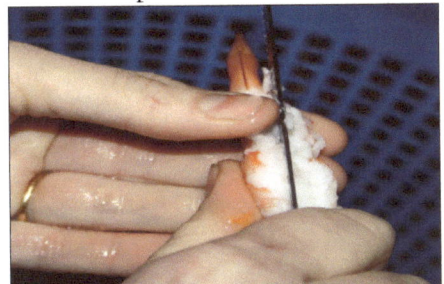

3. ▲ **Butterfly shrimp:** starting near the tail, insert a small knife about half way into the shrimp and continue cutting down to the end of the shrimp. Be careful not to cut completely through. Use your fingers to "open" the shrimp so that it lays flat.
4. In a small bowl whisk eggs and salt.
5. Spread flour on a plate.
6. Place coconut in a separate bowl.

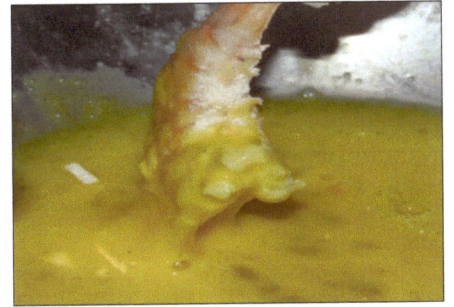

7. ▲ Holding the shrimp by the tail, dip in the egg mixture.

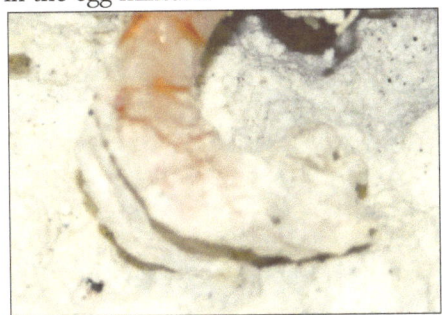

8. ▲ Then dredge in the flour.

9. ▲ Finally dip in the coconut.

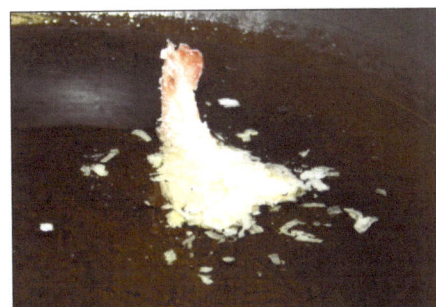

10. ▲ Heat oil in a fry pan or wok on high heat. When hot, carefully place shrimp in the oil. Fry for 2 minutes, or until golden brown. Continue frying until all the shrimp are done. Avoid cooking more than 10 shrimp at a time as it will increase cooking time and soften shrimp.
11. Transfer to a serving plate and serve at room temperature.
Serves 4-6.

Singapore

Curried Shrimp in a Sauce

Ingredients
4 pounds shrimp
½ cup vegetable oil
1 large onion, thinly sliced
2 large chopped tomatoes
1 chopped green chili pepper
1 tablespoon curry powder
1 teaspoon garam masala powder
   (available at Indian grocery stores)
1 ½ teaspoon salt
¾ cup water
½ cup minced cilantro

Preparation
1. **Devein the shrimp** (if necessary): remove shrimp veins with your fingers or a small knife. Rinse shrimp in a strainer.
2. **Prepare curry sauce:** warm oil in a frying pan over medium heat. Add onions and sauté until transparent. Add the tomatoes and green chilies. Sauté together until the tomatoes are soft.
3. Add curry powder, *garam masala*, and salt. Sauté for 1-2 minutes.
4. Stir in shrimp and mix well. Stir in water. Cook together for about 7 minutes.
5. Remove pan from heat. Mix in cilantro.
6. Serve hot.

Serves 6-8

Curried Coconut Shrimp

Far East

Ingredients
2 pounds large shrimp
½ cup cornmeal
1/3 cup water
½ cup coconut milk
1 beaten egg
½ teaspoon salt
1 cup shredded coconut
½ cup flour
vegetable oil (for frying)

Curry Sauce
1 tablespoon corn oil
2 cloves chopped garlic
1 tablespoon sugar
½ tablespoon salt
1 ½ tablespoons curry powder
2 teaspoons cornmeal
1 cup chicken stock (or 1 bullion cube dissolved in 1 cup of hot water)
¾ cup coconut milk
2 tablespoons heavy cream
2 tablespoons lemon juice

Preparation
1. Wash and shell shrimp. Leave tail on.
2. **Butterfly shrimp:** starting near the tail, insert a small knife about half way into the shrimp and continue cutting down to the end of the shrimp. Be careful not to cut completely through. Use your fingers to "open" the shrimp so that it lays flat. Refer to **Coconut Shrimp** recipe for picture.
3. **Devein shrimp:** remove shrimp veins with your fingers or a small knife. Rinse shrimp in a strainer.
4. In a bowl, mix cornmeal and flour. Dredge shrimp in the cornmeal and flour.
5. In a separate bowl mix water, coconut milk, egg, and salt. Whisk until smooth. Stir in shredded coconut. Mix well. Dip the shrimp in the coconut batter.
6. Heat oil in a fry pan or wok on high heat. When hot, carefully place shrimp in the oil. Fry for 2 minutes, or until golden brown. Continue frying until all the shrimp are done. Avoid cooking more than 10 shrimp at a time as it will increase cooking time and over-soften shrimp.
7. **Prepare curry sauce:** Heat oil on medium-high heat. Add garlic and sauté until golden brown. When garlic is golden, mix in sugar, salt, and curry powder. Stir for one minute.
8. In a small bowl, mix cornmeal and chicken stock. Stir into garlic and curry.
9. Add coconut cream. Stir constantly until it boils and thickens. Stir in heavy cream and lemon juice.
10. Use the curry sauce as a dipping sauce or drizzle over shrimp.
11. Serve immediately, at room temperature.
Serves 2-4.

Fish Sauces

Garlic and Lemon Dipping Sauce
Lebanon
Toom ma'al hamood

Ingredients
2 tablespoons garlic paste
1 cup lemon juice
¼ cup olive oil
½ teaspoon salt

Preparation
1. In a medium-bowl, mix the garlic, lemon juice, olive oil, and salt.
2. Serve at room temperature alongside fish.

Tahini Dipping Sauce
Lebanon
Tarratoor

Ingredients
2 tablespoons garlic paste
1 cup lemon juice
½ cup *Tahini* (available at Middle Eastern stores)
½ teaspoon salt

Preparation
1. In a medium-bowl, mix the garlic, lemon juice, tahini, and salt.
2. Serve at room temperature alongside fish or **Fried Kibbeh** recipe in **Meat Chapter**

Stuffed Vegetables Chapter

Hajjah Naziha and the Stuffed Cucumber

One day when Hajjah Naziha was young, around 10 years old, she asked her mother, Hajjah Amina ق, if she could cook in the kitchen. That day the ladies in the kitchen were preparing one of the myriad of dishes which involve coring the zucchini. Hajjah Amina replied, "No, you might break the zucchini." Hajjah Amina was extremely busy and didn't have time to teach her daughter. She cooked two meals a day for the students of Grandshaykh Abdullah Daghestani ق. She was responsible for feeding a large number of people, in addition to taking care of her children and doing the wash.

The young Naziha was disappointed, but she understood how busy her mother was, and tried to be patient. So, she went to sit on a stone staircase outside. As she left the kitchen she took a cucumber and a vegetable corer. She was holding a cucumber, and pressing into it with a corer, pretending that it was a zucchini she was coring. She ate the inside of the cucumber as she cored it.

Hajjah Naziha's father, H.E. Mawlana Shaykh Nazim ق, passed her as he was walking. He saw her with the corer and cucumber. He smiled and asked her, "What are you doing?" Naziha replied, "I am pretending this cucumber is a zucchini and I am coring it. My mother wouldn't let me core zucchini in the kitchen." Her father looked at her for a little while. He said to her, "Come my dear." He took her by the hand to her mother in the kitchen, and said, "I found Naziha outside playing with a cucumber pretending it's a zucchini. Let her help in the kitchen."

Hajjah Amina told her husband she would teach Naziha. She took Naziha into the kitchen and showed her how to core zucchini. She was very surprised that her daughter didn't break any zucchini; even though it was her first attempt. It turned out that Naziha had been practicing by herself with a cucumber for quite a while, and was already quite proficient at coring.

This story shows the respect the family members had for each other. The young Hajjah Naziha had respect for her mother. Even when it was difficult, she didn't whine and cry. It also demonstrates the respect that H.E. Mawlana Shaykh Nazim ق had for his daughter's desire to learn. His attention to Hajjah Naziha's desire to help in the kitchen seems to foreshadow her great skill as a cook. Lastly, it shows the great respect that Hajjah Amina had for her husband; she listened to him when he told her to teach their daughter. In the end, Hajjah Naziha's cored and stuffed cucumber lay beside the zucchini when the finished dish was served!

Mediterranean
Arnabeet Mahshee

Whole Cauliflower Stuffed with Ground Beef

Ingredients
1 whole head cauliflower
½ pound ground beef
1 small onion, finely chopped
1 teaspoon salt
½ teaspoon pepper
½ teaspoon cinnamon
1 tablespoon butter
2 tablespoons pine nuts
1 cup vegetable oil (for frying)

Preparation
1. Preheat oven to 400°F.
2. Remove stems and leaves from cauliflower.
3. In a large pot, bring water to a boil over high heat. Place cauliflower in pot.
4. Boil the cauliflower whole for approximately 10 minutes, or until slightly soft but still very firm.
   Note: If the cauliflower is cooked too long, it will fall apart when stuffed.
5. Remove cauliflower from water with a large slotted spoon and fork. Set aside to cool.
6. **Prepare the filling:** cook the ground beef and onion over medium-high heat in a skillet until the meat releases its own juices. Add the salt, pepper, and cinnamon. Continue cooking until meat is dark brown.
7. In a small saucepan, melt the butter over medium-low heat. Add pine nuts and sauté until golden brown. Mix the pine nuts and any pan drippings into the ground beef mixture.

8. ▲ Stuff the cauliflower using your fingers and a teaspoon to put the ground beef mixture between the florets, being careful not to break it. Then turn cauliflower over and try to add a little more filling between the front florets.

9. ▲ Heat oil in a wok or round fry pan over medium-high heat. Once oil is hot, add cauliflower, top down. Start to brown. Then, using a spatula, hold cauliflower on its side and brown all the way around the cauliflower.
10. Fry the bottom. Once it is brown, place in a baking dish and bake for about 20 minutes.
11. Serve hot.

Serves 4-6

Bosnia
Luk Dolma

Stuffed Onions

Ingredients
8 medium onions
3 cups water
1 teaspoon white vinegar

Filling
1 pound ground beef
1 grated small onion
9 grated baby carrots
½ cup short grain rice
1 grated medium tomato, discard skin
2 ½ teaspoons salt
¼ teaspoon pepper
¼ teaspoon paprika
1 teaspoon olive oil
¼ cup water

Sauce
2 tablespoons olive oil
2 small onion centers
1 small plum tomato, finely chopped
1 teaspoon flour
½ teaspoon paprika
¼ teaspoon salt
2 cups water

To Cover
1 tomato, cut into pieces

Preparation
1. Peel onions. Cut ½-inch off of the tops and bottoms. Place onions in a pot.
2. Add 3 cups water and vinegar to pot. Bring to a boil over high heat. Reduce heat to medium-high and boil for 20 to 40 minutes, depending on type of onion. They should be soft, but not so cooked that they will crumble. When ready, the onion color will change; from white to yellowish.
3. Drain onions and set aside until cool enough to handle.

4. ▲ Over a tray, gently squeeze the onions, one at a time, so the centers pop out. Set aside onion centers. What remains will be the onion "shell;" used for stuffing. Set onion shells upright on a tray. Onions vary greatly; some rip more than others. If the onion shells break, use two layers of the onion to form a single shell.
5. **Prepare filling:** to a bowl add ground beef, grated onion, grated carrots, rice, grated tomatoes, salt, pepper, paprika, oil, and water. Mix well.

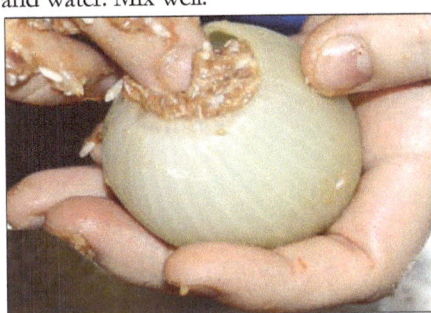

6. ▲ Stuff the onion shells gently with the filling, being careful not to break them.
7. **Prepare sauce:** Chop 2 of the small onion centers. Heat 2 tablespoons olive oil in a saucepan on high heat. Sauté onion centers and plum tomatoes. Add flour, paprika, and salt. Add ½ a cup of water and bring to boil. Remove from heat.

8. ▲ Gently place stuffed onions in the pot. Spoon half the sauce over the onions. Gently and slowly add the rest of the sauce from the side of the pot. Add remaining 1 ½ cups water from the side of the pot. Cover the top of the stuffed onions with the cut tomato. Cover the pot with its lid. Bring to a boil on high heat. Reduce heat to medium-low and continue boiling, covered, for 45 minutes.
9. Transfer to a serving dish.
10. Serve hot with plain yogurt or sour cream.

Serves 4-6

Cyprus
Etli Enginar Dolması

Artichokes Stuffed with Seasoned Ground Beef

Ingredients
4 medium-sized artichokes
¼ cup vegetable oil
½ teaspoon salt

Filling
1 pound ground beef
1 onion, finely chopped
1 ½ teaspoons salt
½ teaspoon pepper
½ teaspoon cinnamon
½ bunch chopped parsley

Sauce
3 cups hot water
1 ½ teaspoons salt
1 teaspoon lemon juice

Preparation
1. Preheat oven to 425°F.
2. **Prepare the filling:** cook the ground beef and onion over medium-high heat in a skillet until meat releases its juices. Add salt, pepper, and cinnamon. Continue cooking until meat is dark brown. Stir in parsley. Set aside to cool.

3. ▲Remove outer bottom leaves. Cut off stem so artichoke is "flat." Artichoke should be able to sit by itself.

4. ▲Cut off top inch of artichoke.

5. ▲Core center of artichoke; remove inner lighter-colored leaves.

6. ▲ With a spoon, scrape away inside of artichoke. Scrape out all the white feathery part from inside. A lot of fuzzy hair, or "choke" will come out from inside. Some artichokes have more "choke" than others. After removing "choke;" wash artichokes thoroughly with water and place upside-down on a flat surface, a plate or tray lined with paper towel.

Note: If preparing several artichokes, better to wear disposable gloves. Your hands will become blackened if you don't. If they become blackened, use a lemon cut in half to remove the stain.

7. ▲ Heat vegetable oil in a pot with ½ teaspoon salt on high heat. When hot, add artichokes and fry the bottom for 5 minutes or until golden-brown.

8. ▲ Remove from oil and place in 8-inch x 8-inch baking dish.

9. ▲ Fill artichokes, using a teaspoon and your fingers, with ground beef filling. Fill almost to top. Return stuffed artichokes to baking pan. If there is excess filling, serve on the side.

10. **Prepare sauce:** mix water, salt, and lemon juice. It is very important to pour sauce in from the corner of the baking dish so the meat filling won't spill out of the artichokes.

11. Cover with aluminum foil. Bake for 1 hour and 30 minutes, or until the artichoke leaves pull off easily.

12. Serve hot.

Serves 2-4

Syria
Shaykh al-Mahshee

Stuffed Zucchini in Yogurt Sauce

Ingredients
13 Arab zucchini (available at Middle Eastern stores)
1 pound ground beef
1 small onion, finely chopped
2 teaspoons salt
1 teaspoon pepper
1 teaspoon cinnamon
2 tablespoons butter
½ cup pine nuts
1 cup vegetable oil (for frying)

Sauce
2 pounds (32 ounces) plain yogurt
3 cups water
2 teaspoons salt
1 tablespoon cornstarch
2 egg whites

Tools

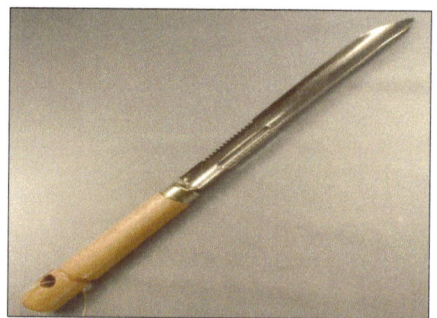

▲ To properly "core," or remove the insides, it is useful to purchase a special vegetable corer, as shown above (available at Middle Eastern stores).

1. ▲ Cut the tops off of zucchini.

Preparation

2. ▲ Thinly slice off the bottom.

3. ▲ First, measure the corer against the zucchini (as shown above) to get the right length.

4. ▲ Insert corer into top of zucchini.

5. ▲ Start to core by making a small circle.

6. ▲ Widen the opening. Gently turn to remove the insides. Be careful not to break the zucchini or poke holes in them while coring.

7. ▲ Properly cored zucchini. Continue until all zucchini are cored. Reserve the insides of the zucchini in a separate bowl.

Note: You can use the insides of the zucchini to prepare the **Zucchini Salad** recipe in the **Salad Chapter**. Rinse cored zucchini.

8. **Prepare filling:** cook ground beef and onion over medium-high heat in a skillet until the meat releases its own juices. Add salt, pepper, and cinnamon. Continue cooking until meat is dark brown.
9. In a small saucepan, melt 1 tablespoon of the butter over medium-low heat. Add ¼ cup of the pine nuts and sauté until golden brown. Mix the pine nuts and any pan drippings into the ground beef mixture. Let cool.
10. Stuff zucchini with meat mixture, using your index finger to press the meat gently inside zucchini. Be careful not to overstuff zucchini or they will break.
11. Warm oil in a large pot over medium-high heat. When hot, add zucchini and fry 5 or 6 at a time.
12. Fry stuffed zucchini until dark golden brown.

13. ▲ Remove from oil and place in a strainer (with a paper towel underneath to absorb any excess oil).

14. ▲ Separate egg whites.
15. **Prepare sauce:** warm a large, deep pot over high heat. Add yogurt, water, salt, cornstarch, and egg whites. Mix well. Bring to a boil, stirring occasionally. Once the yogurt starts to boil, reduce heat to medium-low.

16. ▲ Gently add stuffed zucchini to yogurt sauce. Do not place zucchini on top of each other in the pot. Place gently in an empty place in the yogurt sauce until all of the zucchini are added. Let simmer in yogurt sauce for 15-20 minutes.

Note: The zucchini will turn the yogurt slightly yellow.

17. Transfer zucchini and yogurt to a large serving dish: pick up zucchini one at a time with a slotted spoon and place on dish. Spoon the yogurt sauce over zucchini.
18. In a small saucepan, melt the remaining tablespoon of butter over medium-low heat. Add remaining ¼ cup of pine nuts and sauté until golden brown.
19. Decorate top of zucchini in serving dish with the pine nuts and butter.
20. Serve hot.

Serves 8

Lebanon
Mahshee Mashkal

Stuffed Grape Leaves, Eggplant, & Zucchini

Hajjah Yousra, Hajjah Naziha's mother-in-law, taught her to prepare this dish. To properly "core," or remove the insides, from the zucchini and eggplants it is good to use a vegetable corer, available at Middle Eastern stores. The sauce that the vegetables are cooked in is served alongside the completed dish.

Ingredients
7 Arab eggplants (available at Middle Eastern stores)
8 Arab zucchini (available at Middle Eastern stores)
8 ounces (half of a 16-ounce jar) grape leaves
1 ¼ pounds ground beef
2 ¼ cups short grain rice
2 small onions, finely chopped
2 ½ tablespoons salt
1 teaspoon pepper
1 ½ teaspoons cinnamon
¾ cup water

Sauce
1/3 cup tomato paste
1 teaspoon salt
10 cups water
½ head crushed garlic
¼ cup lemon juice
1 tablespoon dried mint
2 ½ tablespoons butter

Preparation
1. **Prepare grape leaves:** drain and rinse leaves with cold water. Soak leaves in a large bowl of warm water to remove bad taste from jar. Rinse in a strainer.

2. ▲ **Prepare zucchini and eggplant:** cut ends off of zucchini and eggplant.

3. ▲ Gently core the vegetables, using an Arab vegetable corer, to remove the insides. Be careful not to break the vegetables or poke holes in them. To read further about coring and stuffing zucchini refer to **Stuffed Zucchini in Yogurt Sauce**.

Note: Gently place your little finger inside the zucchini to make sure the inside has been adequately removed at the bottom. If you don't do this, sometimes you end up with a lot of the filling at the top of the vegetables and no filling at the bottom.

4. **Prepare filling:** mix ground beef, onions, rice, salt, pepper, cinnamon, and ¾ cups water in a bowl.

5. **Stuff the cored zucchini and eggplant**: Gently shake the zucchini and eggplant and press with your little finger on the top of the filling to make sure the filling goes in properly.

6. Once all the vegetables are stuffed, place in a large pot and stand them upright.

7. ▲ **Prepare grape leaves to stuff:** The leaves have 2 different sides. One side is heavily veined, and one side is smooth, or "shiny." Take a leaf and put the smooth, shiny-side down on the counter. Cut off the stem from end of grape leaf.

8. ▲ Place one tablespoon of filling at the bottom of the leaf.

9. ▲ Fold the bottom of the leaf over the filling.

▲ Fold a side of the leaf on top of the covered filling.

9. ▲ Fold the other side of the leaf on top of the filling to prepare for rolling.

10. ▲ Begin rolling, tightly but not so much as to cause it to break. Roll the grape leaves so they are about 2 inches long and a ½-inch wide.

11. ▲ Once all the grape leaves are rolled, lay a thread across a plate and begin stacking the dolmas on top of the thread. Place about 5 or 6 dolmas down then start stacking them on top of each other till they are about 5-6 rows high.

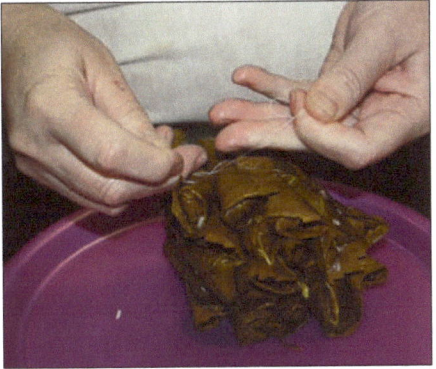

12. ▲ Then tie a knot. Be careful not to pull the string too tight because it will cut the dolmas in half. Then carefully flip over and tie again. (If the grape leaves are not tied they will open while cooking.) Place in the middle of the pot, with the zucchini and eggplant "standing" around them, filling side up. Continue making bundles of grape leaves until finished.

13. **Prepare sauce:** mix tomato paste, salt, water, chopped garlic, lemon juice, and dried mint in a bowl. Mix well and pour over the dolmas. Then cut butter into 1 tablespoon chunks and place in sauce.

14. Cover pot and bring to a boil over high heat. Reduce the heat to medium and boil stuffed vegetables for 40 minutes to 1 hour until zucchini, eggplant, and grape leaves are soft. Use spoon to check zucchini softness by trying to cut through the top. If you can cut with the edge of a spoon, they're done. If not, continue cooking.

15. Serve on an oval or rectangular tray: First remove grape leaves from middle, picking up gently using string. Cut the thread, pull it out, and discard. Place grape leaves in middle of tray. Pick up zucchini and eggplant one by one and place around grape leaves. Set in serving tray in a symmetrical pattern. Reserve sauce left in the pot.

16. Sauce is served in a bowl on the side of the stuffed vegetables.

   Note: Store leftover zucchini, eggplant and grape leaves separate from the sauce.

17. Serve hot.

Serves 6-8

Lebanon
Malfoof Mahshee

Cabbage Leaves Stuffed with Rice & Ground Beef

Ingredients
1 Mediterranean cabbage
1 tablespoon ground cumin
1 pound ground beef
1½ cups short-grain rice
1 teaspoon salt
½ teaspoon pepper
½ teaspoon cinnamon
¼ cup water
½ cup oil

Sauce
6 ½ cups water
6 tablespoons tomato paste
3 tablespoons salt
2 tablespoons dried mint
2 tablespoons garlic
¼ cup lemon juice
6 tablespoons butter

Preparation

1. ▲Remove and discard outer leaves.
2. Put cabbage in a large pot. Add water to cover ¾ of the cabbage. Remove cabbage from pot. Bring water to a boil over high heat. Add cumin to the water. (Cumin reduces cabbage's gaseous properties).
3. Place another large bowl, full of cold water, next to the pot of boiling water. When the water boils, place the whole cabbage, stem up, in the pot.

4. ▲Start to cut the outer layer of cabbage leaves, as shown above. Hold the stem with one hand and cut 4-5 leaves with your other hand.

5. ▲Boil cut leaves in the pot until firm but soft.

6. ▲Remove soft leaves from boiling water, and place in the bowl of cold water.

7. ▲Leave leaves in cold water for 2-3 minutes. The water will warm as you add the hot cabbage leaves, so periodically pour out water and fill back up with cold water.
8. When you remove cabbage leaves from bowl, strain in a colander. Continue cutting, boiling and cooling 4-5 leaves at a time untill you are left with a baseball sized "heart." Set this aside.

9. ▲ Leaf on left has been boiled and strained. Leaf on right is raw.

10. ▲ Place each leaf onto a cutting board and devein the cabbage leaves one at a time. To devein, take a small knife and cut out the thick vein that runs up the middle of the leaf.

11. ▲ Then cut the leaf into 2-3 pieces, depending on the size of leaf.
12. Save all the veined pieces you have removed from the leaves. Set aside.
13. **Prepare the filling:** to a bowl add ground beef, rice, salt, pepper, cinnamon, and ¼ cup water. Mix well.

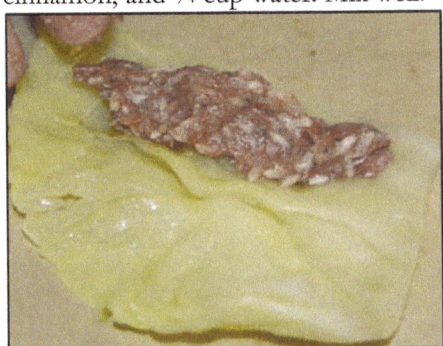

14. ▲ Take about 1 tablespoon of filling and shape it like a small finger. Place on the cabbage leaf.

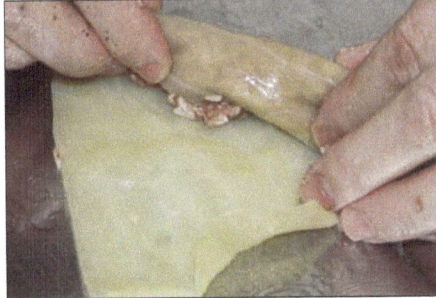

15. ▲ Roll the cabbage leaf like sushi. Roll with the grain of the cabbage. Start with the big side.

16. ▲ Leave the ends of the cabbage open.

17. ▲ Once all the cabbage leaves have been rolled, cut all the saved vein pieces of the cabbage and the heart into 2 inch pieces and place at bottom of a 5-quart pot.

18. ▲ Place the filled cabbage leaves over the cut pieces.

19. ▲ Place a plate upside down over the cabbage rolls and put a bowl filled with water on top of the plate.

Note: The plate and bowl of water keeps the cabbage rolls from becoming unrolled while cooking.

20. ▲ **Prepare sauce:** stir together water, tomato paste, salt, mint, garlic, and lemon juice in a bowl. Mix well. Pour sauce in from side of the pot.

21. ▲ Cut butter into ½-inch pieces. Place in pot, around edges of the plate. Cover and bring to a boil over high heat. Once it boils, reduce heat to medium-high.
22. Remove bowl of water, but keep plate. After boiling 10-15 minutes, remove plate. Reduce heat to low and simmer for 50 minutes. Check for doneness: If rice is tender, it's done. If not, continue cooking.
23. Serve hot.

Serves 8-10

Lebanon
Silaq Mahshee

Stuffed Swiss Chard

Ingredients
2 pounds chard
1 pound ground beef
2 teaspoon salt
1 teaspoon pepper
¾ cup short grain rice
1 teaspoon cinnamon
¼ cup water

Sauce
3 cups water
½ cup lemon juice
¼ cup + 1 ½ tablespoons butter
1 teaspoon salt

Preparation
1. Mix ground beef, rice, ¼ cup water, salt, pepper and cinnamon in a bowl.

2. ▲ Cut the stems off chard leaves.

3. ▲ Fill a large pot half way with water.

Bring to a boil. Blanch 5-6 leaves at a time, boiling between 2-3 minutes or till they change to a bright green.

Note : Keep watching leaves. Don't leave them more than five minutes in the water or they will be too soft.

4. ▲ Immediately place blanched leaves in a bowl of cold water. Since the leaves are hot and will warm the water, keep changing the water to cold water, for the next batch of leaves. Place cooled leaves in a plate. Repeat till all leaves are finished.

5. ▲ Place a blanched leaf, bumpy side up, on a cutting board. Make the first cut roughly 4 inches from the broader end of the leaf.

6. ▲ Continue cutting chard leaves as illustrated. Cutting out and saving the thick white spine for later.

Note: Chard leaves come in varyingsizes. Some leaves yield three pieces, while some can yield five pieces. Each piece should be roughly 6 inches by 4 inches.

7. ▲ Shape filling to a finger shape and place it about ½ inch away from the edge of the leaf.

8. ▲ First fold the ½ inch edge over the filling and then fold both sides of the leaf in.

9. ▲ Begin rolling tightly from folded edge. Roll to end of leaf.

10. ▲ Keep stacking rolled leaves on a plate, until all are rolled.

11. ▲ Place some of the chard "spines", on the bottom of a large pot. (Save the rest for the **Chard Stem and Yogurt** recipe in the vegetable chapter). Place the rolled leaves on top, arranging in an alternating direction.

12. ▲ Stack loosely till all of them are stacked in the pot.

13. ▲ Cover them with an inverted plate, that fits in the pot.

14. ▲ Place a bowl half filled with water on top of plate. Mix the 3 cups water, lemon juice and salt in a bowl. Pour it in the side of the pot. (Not in the bowl of water). Slice the butter and sprinkle around the sauce.
15. Cover pot and bring to a boil. Once it boils, remove lid and reduce to low. Cook for 45 minutes or until rice is cooked. Some sauce will remain.
16. Leave to set for five minutes.
17. Stack them one by one on a plate.
18. Serve hot, accompanied with **Chard Stem and Yogurt** from vegetable chapter.
Serves 2-4

Lebanon
Bataata mahsheeah bil-Lahmah al-Mafroomah

Ground Beef Stuffed Golden Potatoes

Hajjah Yousra, Hajjah Naziha's mother-in-law, taught her to prepare this dish.

Ingredients
15 medium potatoes, peeled (use uniform type)
2 cups vegetable oil (for frying)
1 ½ pounds ground beef
1 medium onion, finely chopped
2 teaspoons salt
1 teaspoon pepper
1 teaspoon cinnamon
1 tablespoon butter
¼ cup pine nuts

Sauce
4 cups water
3 tablespoons tomato paste
¼ cup lemon juice
1 teaspoon salt

Preparation
1. Preheat oven to 400°F.

2. ▲ Core each potato; remove insides using a vegetable corer.

3. ▲ Warm oil in a pot over high heat. When hot, add cored potatoes and fry until dark golden brown; turning once while cooking to ensure even cooking.
4. Place potatoes in a strainer to drain any excess oil.
5. **Prepare filling:** cook ground beef and onion over medium-high heat in a skillet until the meat releases its juices.
6. Add salt, pepper, and cinnamon. Continue cooking until meat is dark brown.
7. In a small saucepan, melt butter over medium-low heat. Add pine nuts and sauté until golden brown. Immediately mix the pine nuts and any pan juices into the ground beef mixture.
8. Stuff potatoes with meat mixture, using your hands. Gently push filling in with your little finger.
9. Place stuffed potatoes in a 9x13-inch baking dish.
10. **Prepare sauce:** mix water, tomato paste, lemon juice, and salt in a bowl. Mix well and pour into baking dish from the side.
11. Cover and bake for 30 minutes, or until sauce comes to a boil and thickens.
12. Serve hot.

Serves 4-6

Meat Chapter

Kawarma

Hajjah Nazihe relates, "My mother knew how to use everything. She didn't waste anything. When I was 5 or 6 years old, there were no refrigerators where we lived in the Middle East. Every month the butcher would slaughter a sheep for my family. He would skin the animal and then cut it into pieces. My mother would cook the pieces—the meat, the bones, the fat—altogether in a large pot. She would pour salt over the meat, and cook it over low heat for at least 7 hours, until the meat was thoroughly cooked and tender.

She would leave the meat to cool, and then spoon the mixture into special clay jugs. The clay would prevent mold from growing. Then she would cover the mixture with a special thin, white cotton cloth. The fat from the meat would harden and rise to the top. This technique allowed the meat to stay usable for at least six months. The resulting preserved meat is called Kawarma—in Turkish it means cooked over low heat for a long time. Some people still use this technique today."

Lebanon
Kibbeh

Kibbeh Cover Preparation

Kibbeh is a Middle Eastern specialty dish which can be prepared in a variety of different ways; baked, fried, and even eaten raw. Kibbeh consists of a mixture of extremely lean ground beef and Bulgur #3 mixed with different seasonings. The beef has to come from a special grade of beef that has virtually no fat. Also, Bulgur #3 is the smallest size of bulgur. Kibbeh in all its forms is considered a difficult dish to prepare.

Hajjah Naziha presents here a way to make it possible for anyone to successfully prepare Kibbeh. Below is a step-by-step way of preparing the Kibbeh Cover, a key component in the following Kibbeh recipes.

Ingredients
- 2 pounds extra lean ground beef (known as "*kibbeh* meat" at Middle Eastern butchers-special grade of meat)
- 2 pounds Bulgur #3 (the smallest grain of bulgur
- 1 small onion, finely chopped
- 2 tablespoons salt
- ½ teaspoon pepper
- ½ teaspoon cinnamon

Preparation

1. ▲ Rinse bulgur in a large bowl. Drain in fine mesh metal strainer.

2. Drain well, until no more water drips down from strainer. Drain in batches to make sure you get as much water out as possible.

3. Squeeze drained bulgur in your hand to remove any extra water.

4. ▲ Place squeezed bulgur in a bowl with extra lean ground beef.
Mix in salt, pepper, cinnamon, and onion. Mix well.

5. ▲ Take a small amount of the mixture and process in the food processor for about 5 minutes.

6. ▲ When it is thoroughly mixed, it will form a ball in the processor. Keep processing in batches in the food processor. Set processed mixture aside in a bowl. Continue until all the mixture is processed.

This mixture is used in all of the following kibbeh recipes.

Lebanon
Kibbeh Bisinniya bil-Firin

Baked Kibbeh

This is the easiest version of the Lebanese specialty *kibbeh*. Delicious!

Ingredients

Kibbeh Cover
See **Kibbeh Cover Preparation** at the beginning of chapter.

Filling
1 pound ground beef
2 small onions, finely chopped
2 teaspoons salt
1 teaspoon pepper
1 teaspoon cinnamon
2 tablespoons sumac
4 tablespoons butter
1 cup pine nuts
1 tablespoon vegetable oil
3 tablespoons butter

Preparation
1. Preheat oven to 350°F.
2. Prepare *Kibbeh* Cover.
3. **Prepare filling**: to a frying pan add ground beef, onions, salt, pepper, cinnamon, and sumac. Cook over medium-high heat, stirring occasionally, until dark brown.
4. Melt butter in a saucepan over medium-high heat. Add pine nuts and sauté until golden brown. Mix pine nuts and any pan drippings into meat.
5. Grease bottom of a 13 by 15-inch baking dish with vegetable oil.
6. Take some of the *kibbeh* filling and press into the bottom of the baking dish. The lower layer should be ¼-inch thick. Evenly press filling onto the bottom of the baking pan.

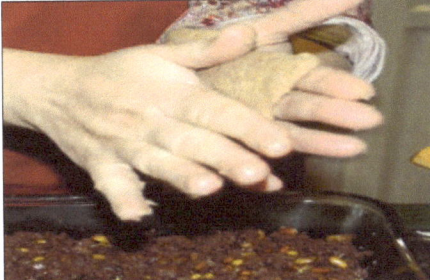

7. ▲ Take small amount of *kibbeh* cover mixture and flatten with your hand to measuring about ¼ inch thick.

8. ▲ Start to patch a layer of kibbeh cover on top of the filling.

Continue until all the filling is covered with wet hands, smooth out cover until even.

9. ▲ Using a sharp knife cut into diamond shapes all the way down to the bottom of the pan. Cut into 4 long rows and then make diagonal cuts across to shape.
10. Melt butter and spoon over the top of the *kibbeh*. Bake uncovered for 1 hour, or until golden brown on top and all sides.
11. Serve hot with salad and yogurt.

Serves 7

Lebanon
Kibbeh Muqlia

Fried Kibbeh

Ingredients

Kibbeh Cover
Kibbeh Cover Preparation at the beginning of chapter.

Filling
1 pound ground beef
2 small onions, finely chopped
2 teaspoons salt
1 teaspoon pepper
1 teaspoon cinnamon
2 tablespoons sumac
2 tablespoons pomegranate paste or molasses (optional; makes filling a bit sour)
1 cup chopped walnuts (optional)

Garnish
chopped parsley leaves

Preparation

1. Prepare *Kibbeh* Cover.
2. **Prepare the filling:** to a frying pan add ground beef, onions, salt, pepper, cinnamon, sumac, and pomegranate paste (optional). Cook over medium-high heat, stirring occasionally, until dark brown. Stir in walnuts.
3. **Form cover mixture for stuffing:** Dip fingers in water to shape cover mixture into an egg-sized, 2-inch ball.

4. ▲ Put your finger in the middle of the ball, be careful not to break the ball with your finger.

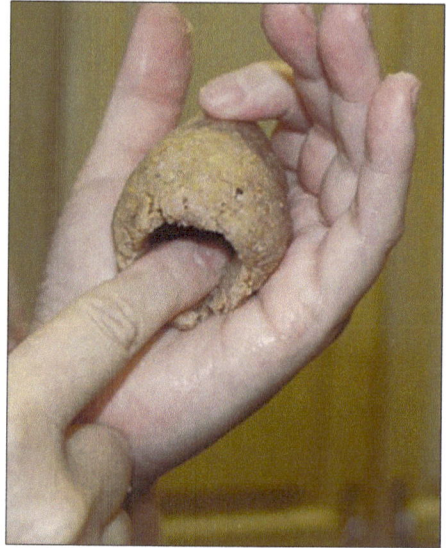

5. ▲ Turn in your hand to widen the opening.

6. ▲ Ready for stuffing.

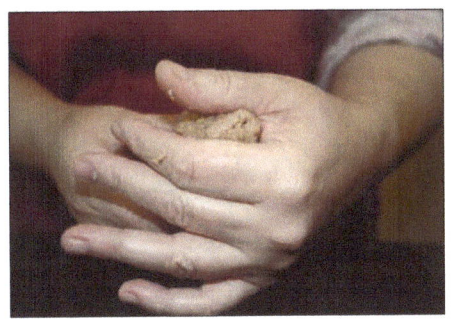
10. ▲ Close the open end.

14. ▲ Heat oil for frying on high heat in a large pan. When hot, add the formed *kibbeh*. Fry, 6-7 at a time, until dark brown, turning to cook evenly.

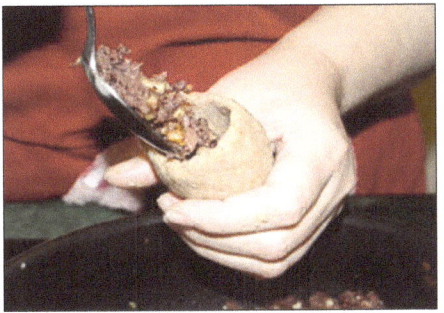
7. ▲ Put a tablespoon of filling into the opening.

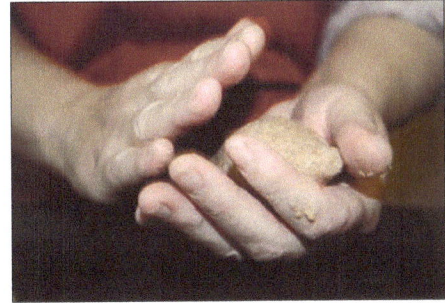
11. ▲ Smooth any cracks that occur with a little bit of water on your fingertips.

15. ▲ Remove from oil with a slotted spoon. Place on a plate lined with paper towel.
16. Place on a serving dish. Garnish with chopped parsley.
17. Makes about 20 fried kibbeh. Serve at room temperature with salad.

Serves 6-8

8. ▲ The filling should not reach all the way to the top.

12. ▲ Filled and shaped kibbeh. Continue to fill and shape the rest.

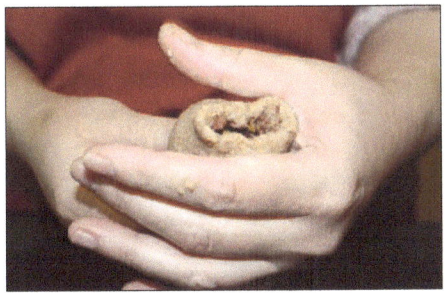
9. ▲ To close the cover around the filling, start by squeezing the sides at the top as you turn in your hands.

13. ▲ As the kibbeh are finished, place on a tray and cover with a towel so they won't dry out.

Lebanon
Kibbeh bil Laban

Filled Kibbeh in Seasoned Yogurt Sauce

Ingredients
Prepare Kibbeh according to **Fried Kibbeh** recipe till step 12 (Previous recipe)

Yogurt sauce
6 pounds plain yogurt
8 cups water

▲ 6 egg whites
2 tablespoons cornstarch
1 head chopped garlic
½ cup chopped cilantro
2 tablespoons butter
¼ cup pine nuts

Preparation
1. **Prepare Fried Kibbeh**: *Kibbeh Muqlia* (previous recipe) but don't fry the kibbeh. The filled kibbeh are added raw to the yogurt sauce. Stop at Step 12 in the preparation for the previous recipe.
2. **Prepare yogurt sauce:** in a large pot, mix yogurt, water, egg white, salt, and corn starch. Mix well and bring to a boil on high heat. Add garlic and cilantro.

3. ▲Slowly add the raw formed *kibbeh* to the yogurt sauce. Don't add the *kibbeh* on top of each other; add them in an empty place in the yogurt sauce. When all the *kibbeh* are in the sauce, cook them for 5 minutes, or until done.
4. Test to see if it's done: Pick up one *kibbeh* and check the ends. If the ends are soft and saturated with yogurt sauce, it's ready.

   Note: Do not overcook or stir *kibbeh*. It will cause them to break and will become mushy in the yogurt.
5. Remove *kibbeh* with a plastic slotted spoon and carefully place in a serving dish, being careful not to break the *kibbeh*. Place next to each other, all on the same level. Don't place on top of each other.
6. Spoon yogurt sauce over *kibbeh*. Melt butter in a saucepan over medium-high heat. Add pine nuts and sauté until golden brown. Sprinkle sautéed pine nuts and butter over yogurt and *kibbeh* in serving dish.
7. Serve at room temperature.
Serves 8-10

Lebanon
Kibbeh Nayyeh

Spicy Raw Ground Beef and Bulgur Mixture

Not for the faint of heart! This dish, prepared with raw meat, must be extremely fresh, and eaten the same day it is prepared.

Ingredients
1 cup Bulgur #3
1 pound extremely fresh, extra lean ground beef (known as "*kibbeh* meat" at Middle Eastern butchers)
1 small onion, finely chopped
1 teaspoon cumin
1 teaspoon cinnamon
1 ½ teaspoons salt
4 teaspoons hot chili powder

Garnish
Decorate with chopped parsley and onions
Drizzle olive oil

Preparation
1. Rinse bulgur in a bowl. Dry in a fine mesh strainer. Squeeze out excess water.
2. To a food processor add: ground beef, bulgur, and onion. Mix for approximately three minutes, or until the mixture forms a ball in the processor. Remove and place in bowl.
3. Knead spices and hot chili into meat mixture.
4. There are 2 ways to serve this dish. One way is to flatten the mixture onto a plate. Decorate with fresh parsley and onions; drizzle with olive oil (shown above). The other way is to shape mixture, by hand, into small, oblong "kibbeh shapes" (like sausages). Place a small bowl of olive oil in the middle of the plate for use as a dipping sauce.

5. ▲ Refrigerate for 30 minutes to 1 hour and serve chilled.

Note: This dish *must* be eaten the same day it is prepared. If there is any left, sauté in a frying pan and eat the next day.

Serves 4-6

Turkey
Pirinçli Köfte

Kofta

Ingredients
6 cups water
1½ cups short-grain rice
2 tablespoons oil
2 small onions, finely chopped
2 pounds ground beef, divided
3 teaspoons salt, divided
2 teaspoons pepper, divided
6 eggs, divided
5 teaspoons dried basil
1 cup flour
2 cups oil (for frying)

Preparation
1. Bring 6 cups water to a boil over high heat. Add rice and boil for 15 minutes, or until rice is tender. Drain rice in a strainer to drain excess water. Rinse with cold water. The rice should be very mushy.
2. Warm oil over high heat. When hot, add onions and sauté until soft. Stir in 1 pound of the ground beef and cook until meat is dark brown. Add 1 teaspoon each of salt and pepper. Set aside to cool.

3. ▲In a separate large bowl, mix remaining 1 pound of raw ground beef, 2 teaspoons salt, 1 teaspoon pepper. Also mix in basil and 1 of the eggs. Mix well. Add the cooked meat and rice to the bowl.

4. ▲Shape *koftas* to be 4-5 inches long and finger-shaped. Roll each *kofta* in the flour. Spread flour evenly on a plate.
5. In a separate bowl scramble 5 of the eggs. Place alongside plate.

6. ▲Dip floured *kofta* in the eggs.

7. ▲Warm oil over high heat. When hot, add breaded *kofta*. Fry until golden brown, 5-6 at a time. Reduce heat to medium so the *kofta* won't burn, and the insides will cook through.
8. Remove with a slotted spoon. Place on a tray or plate lined with paper towel to drain excess oil.
9. Place on a serving plate.
10. Serve at room temperature.

Serves 4-6

Cyprus
Itli Yeshil Bakla

Fresh Fava Beans and Meat Chunks

Ingredients
4 pounds fresh fava beans (available seasonally at Middle Eastern stores)
2 pounds boneless beef chunks or 2 pounds lamb chunks with bones, cut into 1-inch cubes
1 large onion, chopped
6 cups water
1 6-ounce can tomato paste
3 teaspoons salt
½ teaspoon pepper
4 tablespoons lemon juice

Preparation
1. **Prepare fresh fava beans:** Follow directions in **Green Fava Bean Preparation** at beginning of salad chapter on page 12.

2. ▲ Add meat and onions to a pressure cooker or a regular pot. Sauté approximately 10-15 minutes, or until meat is brown, over high heat.
Note: If meat is very lean, add ¼ cup corn oil when sautéing the meat.
3. Add fava beans to meat and onions and stir gently (so you don't break the fava beans) for 5 minutes, or until the color of the pods changes from green to yellowish green.
4. In a bowl, mix water, tomato paste, salt, pepper, and the lemon juice. Stir into meat mixture.
5. **If using a pressure cooker:** close pressure cooker. Bring to a boil over high heat. Once it whistles, reduce heat to medium and cook for 20 minutes, or until meat is tender. Go to last step.
6. **If using a regular pot:** bring to a boil over high heat. Boil on high heat for 10 minutes. Reduce heat to medium-high and boil, partially covered, for 1 hour and 15 minutes, or until fava beans and meat are tender. Check periodically to see if there is enough water for the meat to boil.
7. Serve hot.

Serves 4-6

Lebanon
Yekhni Itil Batata bil Lahme

Cilantro-Flavored Beef Pieces and Potatoes

Ingredients
- 2 pounds meat chunks (beef or lamb), cut into 1-inch cubes
- 10 cups water
- 1 ½ tablespoons salt
- 1 teaspoon pepper
- 1 teaspoon cinnamon
- 1 small onion
- 2 cups oil (for frying)
- 5 pounds potatoes, peeled and cut into 1 ½-inch chunks
- 1 cup minced cilantro
- 2 ½ tablespoons chopped garlic
- ¼ cup lemon juice

Preparation:
1. Place meat, water, salt, pepper, cinnamon and the whole onion in a soup pot. Cover pot and bring to a boil over high heat. Reduce heat to medium-low and cook, partially covered, for 1 hour and 15 minutes, or until meat is tender. Skim off and discard any white foam produced when boiling the meat.
2. Preheat oven to 400°F.
3. Warm oil in a pan over high heat.

4. ▲When hot, add potato chunks and fry until golden brown. Remove with a slopped spoon. Place in baking dish.
5. Remove meat from its broth. Reserve broth. Place meat evenly over potatoes. Mix gently.
6. Stir cilantro, garlic and lemon juice with 3 cups of meat broth in a bowl. Pour evenly over meat and potatoes.
7. Bake uncovered on a low rack for 20-30 minutes, or until sauce boils and thickens. The potatoes will absorb the flavor of the sauce.
8. Serve hot, with rice.

Serves 6-8

Lebanon
Fasulliah Bilahme

Meat with White Beans

Ingredients
1 tablespoon baking soda
24 ounces dry white navy beans
2 pounds beef or lamb chunks, with or without bones, cut to 3/4-inch cubes
Note: meat with bones is more flavorful
15 cups water
1 large onion, finely chopped
1 tablespoon salt
1 teaspoon pepper
1 teaspoon cinnamon

Sauce
4 tablespoons butter
1 head chopped garlic
2 bunches minced cilantro
4 tablespoons tomato paste
½ cup lemon juice

Preparation
1. **Soak beans**: dissolve baking soda in a large bowl of hot water. Add beans. Let sit overnight.
2. In the morning, rinse beans and add to a soup pot with fresh water. Bring to a boil, covered, over high heat. Once the water boils, uncover the pot and reduce the heat to medium. Spoon off and discard any white foam that is produced while cooking the beans. Cook the beans for 40-50 minutes. The beans should be slightly tender, but still a bit hard (they will cook more later with the meat). Strain and rinse in cold water. Set aside.
3. **If using a pressure cooker**: rinse meat and put in a separate pot with 15 cups of water, onion, salt, pepper and cinnamon. Bring to a boil over high heat, or until the pressure cooker whistles. When the water boils, reduce the heat to medium and cook for 20 minutes, or until the meat is tender. Go to Step 5.
4. **If using a regular cooking pot**: rinse meat and put in a pot with 15 cups of water, onion, salt, pepper and cinnamon. Bring to a boil over high heat. When the water boils, reduce the heat to medium and cook, partially covered, for 50 minutes, or until the meat is tender. If the meat produces any foam while cooking spoon off and discard.
5. Melt 4 tablespoons of butter in a skillet. Add garlic and sauté until light golden.

6. ▲ Add cilantro to the garlic. Sauté together until cilantro turns a darker green and becomes soft. Stir in the tomato paste and lemon juice.
7. Put beans in a separate soup pot. Spoon out the meat with a slotted spoon and add to the beans. Add cilantro and garlic mixture.
8. Stir in 4 cups of the meat broth. Bring to a boil, covered, over high heat.
9. When the sauce boils, uncover pot and cook over medium heat for an additional 15-20 minutes, or until sauce is slightly thickened.
Note: Don't stir too much or the beans will become mushy.
10. Serve hot with rice.

Serves 8

Lebanon
Mismisket

Stuffed Biftek

Hajjah Naziha's mother-in-law, Hajjah Yousra, often prepared this specialty dish.

Ingredients
2 pounds thin beef steaks

▲ A specialty known as *biftek* at Middle Eastern butchers.

Note: 2 pounds of *biftek* beefsteak is the equivalent of 12 *biftek* steak pieces as the steaks are small and thin. They should measure 1/16-inch thick and about 4 inches by 6 inches long. Ask your butcher to cut the meat to 1/16-inch thick.

Filling
1 pound ground beef
1 ¼ cups short-grain rice
1 small onion, finely chopped
3 teaspoons salt
1 ½ teaspoons pepper
2 teaspoons cinnamon
¼ cup water
1 tablespoon butter
¼ cup pine nuts
oil (for frying)

Sauce
10 cups water
1 tablespoon salt

Preparation
1. **Prepare filling**: in a bowl mix ground beef, rice, onions, salt, pepper, cinnamon and ¼ cup of water.
2. In a small saucepan melt butter over medium heat. Add pine nuts and sauté until golden brown. Mix pine nuts and butter into filling mixture.

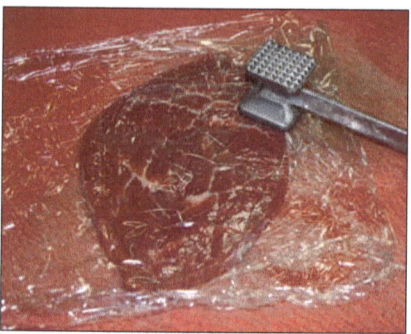

3. ▲**Tenderize steaks with a meat mallet:** put each steak in between 2 pieces of plastic wrap on the counter. Tenderize meat with smooth side of mallet. Start pounding steak gently in center, and then circle out to edges. Continue until all steaks are tenderized. This will make the steaks thinner and wider as they flatten out.

4. ▲ Place ¼ cup of the filling onto each steak.

6. ▲ Biftek stuffed and sewn closed, ready to fry.
7. Warm oil for frying in a pot on high heat.

10. **In a pot add:** meat, water and salt. Bring to a boil on high heat, partially covered. Reduce heat to medium and continue cooking partially covered for one hour, or until meat is tender and rice inside is cooked.
11. When meat is tender, transfer to a serving dish. Ladle sauce from pressure cooker or pot into a gravy bowl to serve alongside. The gravy juices are a flavorful addition to the *biftek*. Before you start eating, pull the string out. It should come out easily.
12. Serve hot.

Serves 8-10

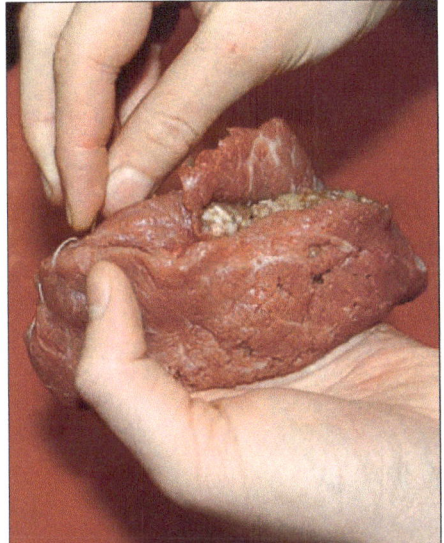

5. ▲ Fold over the steak and then, with white thread (because it has no dyes in it) and a needle, sew the steak closed. Do not pull the thread too tight because it will tear the meat.

8. ▲ When hot, add stuffed *biftek* and fry until brown in color; turn to brown evenly.
9. If cooking in a pot, go to Step 10. **In a pressure cooker add:** meat, water and salt. Bring to a boil, covered, on high heat. When the pressure cooker whistles, reduce heat to medium and cook for 15 minutes.

Cyprus
Köfteli Ekmek Çorbası

Meatballs Over Bread with Yogurt

Hajjah Amina (q) often prepared this dish in Cyprus. It's a delicious way to feed many people with only 2 pounds of meat.

Ingredients
1 ½ pounds country white loaf bread (from bakery), cut into 1-inch cubes

Meatballs
2 pounds ground beef
2 medium onions, finely chopped
1 cup minced parsley
2 teaspoons salt
1 teaspoon pepper
1 teaspoon cinnamon
½ cup vegetable oil
8 cups water
1 tablespoon salt
2 pounds plain yogurt
2 tablespoons butter
1 teaspoon sumac or chili powder

Preparation
1. Place bread cubes in a serving dish.
2. In a large mixing bowl, combine the ground beef, onion, parsley, salt, pepper and cinnamon. Mix well.

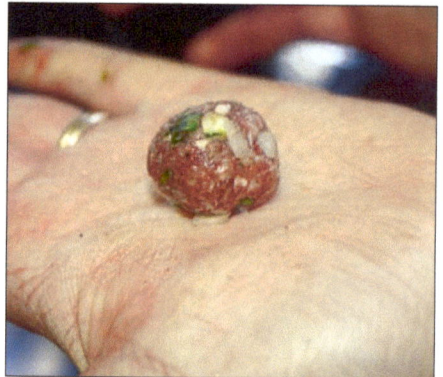

3. ▲ Form into small meatballs, ½-inch in diameter.
4. Warm the oil over high heat.

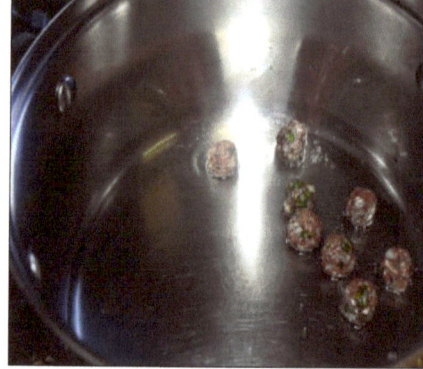

5. ▲ When oil's hot, add formed meatballs and sauté, several at a time, until dark brown. Remove with a slotted spoon and place in a bowl. Set aside. Continue cooking meatballs in batches until all meat is done.
6. When the last batch of meatballs is cooked, leave them in the pot. Also, put back in the pot half of the cooked meatballs, reserving the other half for decoration.

7. ▲ **Prepare sauce**: pour water over meatballs in the pot. Add salt. Bring the sauce to a boil over high heat. Let cook for 10 minutes for the water to absorb the flavor of the meatballs.

8. ▲ Mix the bread chunks with the meatballs and sauce. Mix well.
9. In a small bowl stir the yogurt until smooth.

10. ▲ Evenly pour the yogurt over bread mixture.

11. ▲ Decorate with the reserved meatballs. Place them over the yogurt.
12. In a small saucepan melt the butter. Sprinkle sumac over the yogurt and meatballs. Drizzle with melted butter.
13. Serve hot, immediately.

Serves 10

Cyprus

Musakka

Ingredients
4 pounds eggplant
salt to sprinkle on eggplant
2 cups oil (for frying)
2 cups water
¼ cup lemon juice
1 cup grated mozzarella cheese

Meat
1 ½ pounds ground beef
1 small onion, finely chopped
3 teaspoons salt
1 ½ teaspoons pepper
1 ½ teaspoons cinnamon
¼ cup minced parsley
5 grated plum tomatoes, discard skin

Preparation
1. Preheat oven to 400°F.

2. ▲Peel eggplant in stripes from top to bottom. Slice into ½-inch thick rounds

3. ▲Place in a bowl and sprinkle with salt to draw out eggplant's bitter juices. Let sit for 20 minutes.

4. ▲Gently squeeze eggplant; the bitter juices will come out.
5. Heat oil in a frying pan over high heat.

6. ▲Fry eggplant rounds until golden brown; turning once to ensure even cooking.

7. ▲Place cooked eggplant on tray or plate lined with paper towel to absorb excess oil.

8. ▲ In a separate pan, cook ground beef and onions over medium-high heat until meat is brown, stirring occasionally.

12. ▲ Spread a layer of meat over eggplant.

16. ▲ Mix water and lemon juice in a cup. Slowly pour over eggplant and meat.

9. ▲ Stir in salt, pepper, cinnamon, and parsley.

13. ▲ Cover eggplant completely with the meat.

17. ▲ Sprinkle with mozzarella.
18. Bake uncovered for 30 minutes in a 9x13-inch baking dish, or until top is browned.

Serves 4-6

10. ▲ Mix in grated tomatoes and cook for five more minutes.

14. ▲ Spread remaining half of eggplant over meat.

11. ▲ Place half of the eggplant in a layer on the bottom of a baking dish.

15. ▲ Cover meat with eggplant.

Cyprus
Patatesli Köfte

Potato and Kafta Patties

Ingredients

6 medium potatoes, peeled and grated
2 tablespoons lemon juice

Note: Mix the lemon juice into the grated potatoes so they won't blacken while gathering other ingredients.

2 pounds ground beef
2 onions, finely chopped
1 egg
1½ cups minced parsley
4 teaspoons salt
2 teaspoons pepper
2 teaspoons cinnamon
½ cup bread crumbs
2 cups vegetable oil (for frying)

Preparation

1. ▲ In a large mixing bowl, mix all ingredients, except for the oil

2. ▲ Mix ingredients by hand.

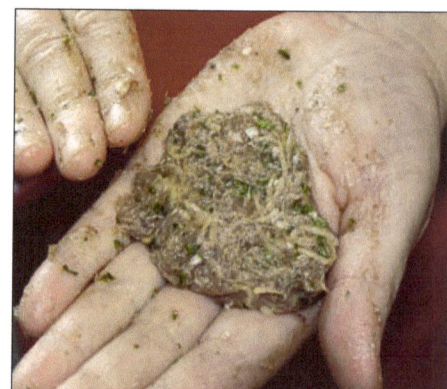

3. ▲ Form into 2 ½-inch round patties (smaller and thinner than a hamburger).

Note: If the patties are falling apart, squeeze out excess liquid and mix in another egg.

4. Warm oil in a frying pan over high heat. When hot, deep fry 7-10 patties at a time, until brown. Fry on each side for five minutes, turning patties over a couple times to cook evenly. Break a patty and check for doneness. If the patties are not cooked in the center, reduce heat and cook longer.
5. Place on plate lined with paper towels to drain excess oil.
6. Serve hot.

Serves 4-6

Lebanon
Kibbetul-Batata bil Firin

Potato and Ground Beef Casserole

Ingredients
Potatoes
5 pounds potatoes
2 ½ cups milk
2 tablespoons salt
¼ cup butter
1 cup bread crumbs, divided

Meat
1 pound ground beef
1 medium chopped onion
2 teaspoons salt
1 teaspoon pepper
1 teaspoon cinnamon
1 tablespoon butter
¼ cup pine nuts

Preparation
1. Place potatoes in a large pot with enough water to cover. Bring to a boil over high heat. Boil potatoes for 20-40 minutes, or until tender.
Note: Always use the same size and type of potatoes so they will have the same cook time.
2. Check for doneness by poking a fork into a potato. If it comes out easily, they are done. If not, boil longer. Drain and rinse with cold water to cool. Peel and roughly chop potatoes.
3. Place potatoes in a bowl. Stir in milk and 2 tablespoons of salt. Mash the potatoes with a hand masher or hand blender until smooth.
4. Brown ground beef and onions over medium-high heat. Mix in salt, pepper and cinnamon.
5. Melt 1 tablespoon of butter in a small saucepan. Add pine nuts and sauté until golden-brown. Add pine nuts and any pan drippings to the meat. Set aside.
6. Melt ¼ cup of butter. Spread butter to coat the bottom of the baking dish. Sprinkle a ½ cup of the breadcrumbs over the butter, tilting the dish to cover evenly.

7. ▲**Prepare the first potato layer**: use half of the potato mixture. Place several spoonfuls of potatoes around the bottom of the dish. Dip a rubber spatula in water and spread the potatoes out to cover the entire bottom of the dish.
Note: Dipping the spatula in water helps to spread the potatoes out easily.
8. Evenly spread all of the meat on top of the first potato layer

9. ▲Spoon the remaining half of the potato mixture over the meat.

10. ▲Again smooth over the top with a rubber spatula.
11. Evenly sprinkle remaining ½ cup of bread crumbs on top. Broil in the oven for 5-10 minutes, or until top is golden brown.
12. Serve hot.
Serves 6-8

Cyprus
Etli Bamia

Okra with Meat

Ingredients
2 pounds okra
1 teaspoon salt
1 cup vegetable oil
1 large onion, finely chopped
4 large tomatoes, chopped or 2 tablespoons tomato paste
1 teaspoon salt
¼ cup lemon juice

Meat Broth
1 pound boneless beef chunks, cut into 1-inch cubes
1 medium onion, quartered
2 teaspoons salt
1 teaspoon pepper
½ teaspoon cinnamon
8 cups water

Preparation

1. ▲ Wash okra. Spread on top of towel to dry.

2. ▲ Lightly peel okra head in a circular shape.

3. ▲ Turn the okra in your hand; the knife should be held in one place with one hand. The other hand should turn the okra from the bottom.

4. ▲ The okra on the left is properly peeled. The okra on the right is cut the wrong way.

Note: Try not to cut into the okra. If cut too deeply, the okra seeds will show. Then the okra dish will be slimy. Also, the moisture from the okra will go into the oil and make it splatter.

5. Heat oil on high heat. Add 1 teaspoon of salt to oil to prevent splattering.

6. ▲ When hot, add okra. Fry until dark green..
7. Remove from heat and strain. Continue frying until all okra is done

8. **Prepare meat broth:** To a separate pot, add meat, onions, salt, pepper, and cinnamon. Add water. Bring to a boil on high heat. Reduce heat to medium and continue to boil, covered, for 45 minutes, or until meat is soft and tender. Spoon off and discard any foam produced when boiling. Set aside.
9. In a separate deep pan, sauté onions with a little oil until transparent. Add tomatoes. Cook together until tomatoes are soft. Add salt and lemon juice.

10. ▲ In an 15 x 10 x 2-inch Pyrex baking dish, place the fried okra.

11. Strain broth. Discard onions. Add strained broth to tomato mixture. Lift meat from the strainer and mix into the tomato mixture.

12. ▲ Pour tomato and meat mixture over okra.
13. Bake, covered, at 400°F for half an hour, or until sauce boils.
14. Serve hot with white rice.

Serves 4-6

Cyprus
Patatesli Biftek

Thin Steaks with French-Fried Potatoes

Ingredients
Meat
2 pounds thin beef steaks (a specialty known as *biftek* at Middle Eastern butchers)
Note: 2 pounds of *biftek* beefsteak is the equivalent of 12 *biftek* steak pieces as the steaks are small and thin. They should measure 1/16 inch thick and about 4 inches by 6 inches long. Ask your butcher to cut the meat to 1/16-inch thick.
1 teaspoon pepper
2 ½ teaspoons salt, divided
½ cup corn oil
Potatoes
8 medium potatoes, peeled and cut into strips
2 cups vegetable oil (for frying)
Sauce
4 cups water
½ cup lemon juice
½ teaspoon dried rosemary
2 teaspoons salt

Preparation
1. Marinate meat overnight in a bowl with pepper and 2 teaspoons of the salt.

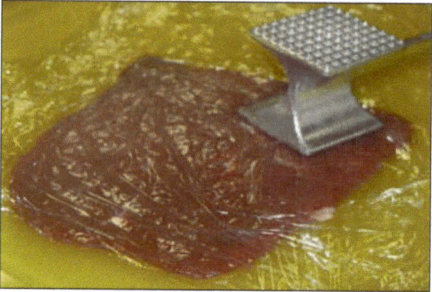

2. ▲ Tenderize steaks with a meat mallet. Put each steak in between 2 pieces of plastic wrap on the counter. Tenderize meat with smooth side of mallet. Start pounding steak gently in center, and then circle out to edges.
3. Preheat oven to 425°F.
4. Heat corn oil in a skillet over medium-high heat. Add a ½ teaspoon of salt to the oil to keep it from splattering.

5. ▲ When oil is hot, add steaks. Fry, two at a time. Brown the first side for three minutes. Flip and brown the other side for two minutes, or until the steaks are a dark brown. Remove from oil and put on a paper towel to drain excess oil.
6. **Prepare potatoes:** Heat oil for frying French fries on high heat. When hot, fry until golden brown. Remove from oil and place on a plate or tray lined with paper towel to drain excess oil.
7. Place steaks on bottom of a 9x13-inch baking dish. Put fried potatoes on top.
8. **Prepare sauce:** mix the water, lemon juice, rosemary and salt in a bowl.
9. Pour sauce over potatoes and meat.
10. Cover with aluminum foil and bake for 40 minutes.
11. Serve hot.
Serves 4-6

Juice and Beverages Chapter

The Importance of Tea

Tea possesses a unique place in Sufi tradition and lifestyle; there are even *qasidas* (devotional songs) which reference the *samovar* (the traditional vessel in which tea is prepared). An old-fashioned *samovar* is an elaborate vessel with a compartment for burning coals at the bottom of an internal tube, which heats the water in the "kettle" section that wraps around it. On top of this is placed a small teapot in which the tea brews over the rising heat. The teapot and tea glasses are filled with boiling water from a tap on the side of a kettle section. It takes water quite some time to boil this way.

Although the *samovar* is still used, most people now prefer the practical, if crude, modern version, which consists of a small tin or enamel teapot, sitting on top of a large tin teapot which in turn is heated over a flame. Electric *samovars* are also commonly used.

There are a number of ways in which tea was, and continues to be, included in Sufi life. Tea is served ritually at a number of crucial points: at the pre-dawn prayer, at the afternoon prayer, and at the breaking of fast.

- ❖ Before the *tahajjud* (pre-dawn) prayer, H.E. Mawlana Shaykh Nazim ق goes to his house to give a special *sohbet*, or lecture. He drinks tea then, before the *fajr* (dawn) prayer. After the *'asr* (afternoon) prayer, he also has tea. These are the times when his teacher, Grandshaykh 'Abdullah Daghestani ق would have tea. Grandshaykh 'Abdullah ق drank tea more than water. Similarly, Hajjah Naziha's maternal grandfather, always drank tea; not water.

- ❖ When Hajjah Naziha was young she would run to Grandshaykh 'Abdullah's ق house after *'asr* prayer. Some of her best memories are of going to his house in the afternoon, sitting and drinking tea. Hajjah Naziha describes these times as "like a Paradise" for her. She would drink tea with her parents and Grandshaykh 'Abdullah ق and his wife. Grandshaykh and his wife led a very simple life. He liked to drink his tea from a *samovar*. In his time, they used the old-fashioned *samovar*, heated with coal.

- ❖ During Ramadan, Hajjah Naziha serves tea every day for *Iftar*, the breaking of the fast. "Tea," she explains, "is remarkably fitting for this in two ways. Firstly, tea helps decrease your thirst. Secondly, it gives you energy." These qualities make tea doubly suitable, not to mention delicious, after a day of fasting.

Turkey
Çay

Black Tea

This tea is traditionally prepared in a samovar and served in glass tea cups, both of which are available at Middle Eastern stores. The samovar consists of a large kettle of boiling water with a small kettle of brewing tea sitting on top. The tea brews in the small kettle from the steam produced from the larger kettle. As the tea from the small kettle is poured out, boiling water from the large kettle is poured in to keep the tea brewing. The tea also stays hot for a long period of time this way.

Ingredients
2 heaping tablespoons good quality tea; such as Earl Grey
Sugar (or Splenda)
Cinnamon stick (optional)

Preparation
1. Put 12 cups of water to boil in the bottom kettle of a samovar. Bring water to boil on high heat.
2. Put tea leaves in small top kettle of samovar. Rinse tea with half a cup of boiling water. Immediately pour out water.
Note: This process of "rinsing" the tea with boiling water helps the tea leaves "open."
3. Pour more boiling water into small kettle from large kettle. Leave 2 inches empty at top of small kettle (so it doesn't boil over). Add the cinnamon stick.

4. ▲ Place small kettle on top of large kettle. If your tea is not good quality, and does not "open," mix ½ teaspoon of sugar into the small pot. Reduce heat to low. The water in the large kettle should be kept at a low boil. Let boil for 2-3 minutes before serving.

5. ▲ To serve the tea, pour some tea (through a strainer) into a glass teacup, about a quarter of the way full.
6. Then, using the boiling water from the large kettle, fill the glass the rest of the way with water. You can adjust the darkness of the tea (some people prefer it light and some prefer it darker) using the samovar. If you add more tea and less water, the tea will be darker. If you add less tea and more water, the tea will be lighter.
7. Fill small back up with boiling water from the large kettle.
8. Serve with sugar.
Serves 6-8

Turkey
Türk Kahvesi

Turkish Coffee

Ingredients
2 Turkish coffee cups of cold water
2 heaping teaspoons Turkish coffee (lighter in color than Arabic coffee)
2 flat teaspoons sugar (to taste)

Preparation
1. **To a Turkish coffeepot add:** water, coffee, and sugar. Mix well.
2. Place coffeemaker on stove on high heat.
3. Bring to a boil. Don't stir. When the coffee foams, spoon some foam into cups, using a teaspoon.
4. Pour coffee into serving cups; the foam will rise to the tops of the cups.
5. Serve hot.
Serves 2

America

SK's Iced Mocha

SK's Regular Iced Mocha

Ingredients

2 teaspoons instant coffee
5 teaspoons unsweetened cocoa powder
8 teaspoons sweetener
1 2/3 cups milk
2 cups ice
prepared whipped cream (for topping)

Preparation

1. **To a blender add:** instant coffee, cocoa powder, sweetener, milk, and ice. Blend until smooth.
2. Divide the mixture evenly into 3 glasses.
3. Top each glass with whipped cream.
4. Serve cold.

Serves 3

SK's Decaffeinated Iced Mocha

Ingredients

3 ½ teaspoons decaffeinated instant coffee
2 tablespoons unsweetened cocoa powder
8 teaspoons sweetener
1 1/3 cups milk
2 cups ice
prepared whipped cream (for topping)

Preparation

1. **To a blender add:** instant coffee, cocoa powder, sweetener, milk, and ice. Blend until smooth.
2. Divide the mixture evenly into 3 glasses.
3. Top each glass with whipped cream.
4. Serve cold.

Serves 3

A sweet, frothy, cold drink which Hajjah Naziha's daughter, Sajeda (SK!), prepares for herself, family, and guests. Inspired by her favorite drink; this is better than what you would find at any coffeeshop (not to mention cheaper!).

Mediterranean
Ayran

Refreshing Yogurt Drink

Ayran is a popular summer drink; the combination of yogurt and mint is incredibly tasty and refreshing in hot weather. This drink was originally prepared from buttermilk so that none of the milk produced when churning butter was wasted. Nowadays it is prepared, as in this recipe, from yogurt and water instead.

Ingredients
2 ½ -3 cups yogurt (depending on how thick you like it)
4 cups water
1 ½ teaspoons salt
½ teaspoon dried mint

Preparation
1. Wisk yogurt in a bowl.
2. Wisk in water, salt, and mint.
3. Pour into a pitcher. Refrigerate.
4. Serve cold.
Serves 6-8

Lebanon
Aseer Burtuqal

Homemade Orange Juice

Hajjah Yousra, Shaykh Hisham's mother, prepared this juice at home. At that time, orange juice wasn't sold in the market.

Ingredients
21 oranges
3 cups sugar
5 cups water

Preparation
1. Cut oranges into chunks (keep the peel on). Pour sugar over orange chunks and cover with plastic wrap. Let sit for 1-2 hours.
2. Place oranges in a strainer over a bowl. Press oranges to squeeze juice out.
3. Pour into a pitcher. Stir in water. Add some ice.
4. Serve chilled.

Serves 6-8

Pineapple Banana

Ingredients
3 cups fresh pineapple
3 medium bananas
2 cups orange juice
½ cup sugar
2 cups water

Preparation
1. **Prepare pineapple:** Remove skin from pineapple. Remove the "eyes" with a knife. Cut pineapple into 4 pieces lengthwise around the core. Discard core. Cut pineapple into chunks. Put the pineapple and its juice into a blender. Blend until smooth.
2. Blend in peeled bananas and orange juice.
3. Add sugar and water. Blend until smooth. Refrigerate.
4. Serve chilled.

Serves 2-4

Ginger Mango Smoothie

Ingredients
8 soft mangos
3 cups yogurt
12 Splenda® packets or 8 tablespoons of either sugar or honey
3 teaspoons ground fresh ginger
1 cup water
1 cup crushed ice (optional)

Preparation
1. Wash and peel the mangos. Slice fruit and discard pits.
2. Blend mango pieces in blender.
3. Add yogurt, water, ginger, and ice (optional).
4. Blend until smooth.
5. Serve chilled.

Serves 4-6

America

Strawberry Milkshake

Ingredients
4 cups whole strawberries
1 cup sugar
3 cups whole milk

Preparation
1. Remove leaves and stems from strawberries.
2. Blend strawberries in a blender on a low setting until smooth.
3. Add milk and sugar. Blend for an additional 2 minutes.
4. Serve chilled.

Serves 3-5

Jam and Preserve Chapter

Traditional Cypriot Jam Making

"The Jams from Cyprus and Turkey are the best I have ever eaten in my entire life." says Hajjah Naziha's daughter-in-law Layla.

At the peak of ripeness and flavor, fruits are harvested, and traditionally preserved in a process that lasts several days. The fruit and sugar are boiled briefly with lemon juice in a pot. The cooked mixture is then spread out in large round trays. The fruit-filled trays are covered with thin white muslin cotton known as "turban cloth." The edges are sealed with clothes pins. The trays are then placed on the rooftop to "cook" under the sun. Obviously, this process is only possible in areas where the sun is very strong, and there is no rain.

The jams are left on the rooftops for 5-7 days. The jam thickens in this way, and the end result has an unbelievably delicious taste. Many bees alight on top of the covered jam, attracted to the fruit and sugar mixture. When Hajjah Naziha was young, between 9-12 years old, it was her job to climb on the roof and stir the jam once a day. When she came to stir the jam, the bees would alight on her, oftentimes stinging her.

In this section, Hajjah Naziha presents another method for preparing jam, which is also delicious. Further, it is not as time consuming and is free of bee stings. Whichever fruit you choose to preserve (whatever is seasonal and plentifully available), is boiled with sugar and lemon juice. Lemon juice is added to prevent the sugar from crystallizing in the jars. The fruit pieces cook for a while, and are then removed with a slotted spoon so just the fruit juices continue to boil with the sugar and water.

A white foam will be produced when boiling the fruit juices. This foam should be spooned off and discarded or possibly used in another way. For instance, Hajjah Amina ق, who didn't like to waste, would keep the foam. She would use the foamy liquid as a fruity concentrate; i.e. mix it with water to make a delicious drink.

Cooking the juices helps thicken the jam. However, if it is done too long the juices and sugar may burn, resulting in a bad taste. Thus, fruit pectin may also be used to help thicken the jam. In the end, the fruit is added back to the juice, and spooned into glass canning jars. The end result is a delicious, homemade jam. *Sahtein—bon appetit!*

Middle East
Mrabal Mish Mish

Golden Apricot Jam

Ingredients

4 pounds apricots, unpeeled and cut into 8-pieces each
4 cups sugar
1 tablespoon lemon juice
1.75 ounce box fruit pectin (if needed to help thicken)

Preparation

1. Pour sugar evenly over apricot pieces in a large bowl. Cover bowl with plastic wrap. Refrigerate overnight, or for at least 12 hours.

2. ▲ In the morning, the fruit will have released a lot of juice into the sugar. There may still be some undissolved sugar in the bowl.
3. Pour the fruit, sugar, and liquid from the bowl into a pot. Bring to a boil over high heat. Reduce heat to medium and continue boiling, uncovered, stirring occasionally. Boil apricots for 8 minutes, or until softened.

4. ▲ Remove fruit with a slotted spoon and place cooked fruit into a strainer inside a large bowl.
5. Mix lemon juice into the juices left in the pot. Continue cooking, uncovered, on low-medium heat.

6. ▲ A white foam will develop, especially around the sides of the pot. Spoon off foam and discard. It's very important to use a dry spoon when doing this.
7. Whatever juice strains into the bowl from fruit in the strainer, pour back into juice boiling in the pot.
8. Continue boiling juice, uncovered, stirring occasionally until juice thickens to the consistency of maple syrup.

Note: Test to see if syrup is ready: refrigerate a small plate for ½ hour before testing. Take a tablespoon of juice and place on plate. The juice should cool quickly on the refrigerated plate. Check with your finger how thick juice is when cool. If the juice thickens when cool to the consistency of maple syrup, it's ready. If you lift it with a spoon, it should stick to the spoon, not drop like water.

9. Go to **Jam Sealing Instructions** at end of chapter.

Makes 2 16-ounce jars.

Turkey
Kiraz Reçeli

Cherry Jam

Ingredients
- 10 cups sugar
- 5 pounds whole cherries
- 3 cups water
- 5 tablespoons fresh lemon juice
- 1.75 ounce box fruit pectin (if needed to help thicken)

Preparation
1. Place whole cherries in a stainless steel pot. Cover with sugar. Let sit overnight.
2. In the morning, heat cherries and sugar on medium-high heat. Mix in the water.

3. ▲Let cook together for 20-30 minutes; then remove cherries with a slotted spoon. Place cooked fruit into a strainer inside a large bowl.
4. Mix lemon juice into the juices left in the pot. Continue cooking, uncovered, on low-medium heat for half an hour.

5. ▲A white foam will develop, especially around the sides of the pot. Spoon off foam and discard. It's very important to use a dry spoon when doing this.
6. Whatever juice strains into the bowl from fruit in the strainer, pour back into juice boiling in the pot.
7. Continue boiling juice, uncovered, stirring occasionally until juice thickens to the consistency of maple syrup.

Note: Test to see if syrup is ready: Refrigerate a small plate for ½ hour before testing. Take a tablespoon of juice and place on plate. The juice should cool quickly on the refrigerated plate. Check with your finger how thick juice is when cool. If the juice thickens when cool to the consistency of maple syrup, it's ready. If you lift it with a spoon, it should stick to the spoon, not drop like water.

8. Go to **Jam Sealing Instructions** at end of chapter.

Makes 2 16-ounce jars.

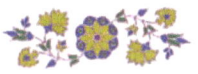

Middle East
Mrabul Tifah

Apple Jam

Ingredients
- 4 pounds apples, peeled and cut into small pieces.
- 4 cups sugar
- 1 tablespoon lemon juice
- 1.75 ounce box fruit pectin (if needed to help thicken)

Preparation
1. Pour sugar evenly over apple pieces in a large bowl. Cover bowl with plastic wrap. Refrigerate overnight, or for at least 12 hours.
2. In the morning, the fruit will have released a lot of juice into the sugar. There may still be some undissolved sugar in the bottom of the bowl.

3. ▲Pour the fruit, sugar and liquid from the bowl into a pot.
4. Bring to a boil over high heat. Reduce heat to medium and continue boiling, uncovered, stirring occasionally. Boil apples for one hour, or until softened.
5. Remove fruit with a slotted spoon and place cooked fruit into a strainer inside a large bowl.
6. Mix lemon juice into the juices left in the pot. Continue cooking, uncovered, on low-medium heat. Remove from heat. After you add the lemon juice, don't leave the pan because then the juices can burn very quickly.
7. A white foam will develop, especially around the sides of the pot. Spoon off foam and discard. It's very important to use a dry spoon when doing this.
8. Whatever juice strains into the bowl from fruit in the strainer, pour back into juice boiling in the pot.
9. Continue boiling juice, uncovered, stirring occasionally until juice thickens to the consistency of maple syrup.

Note: Test to see if syrup is ready: refrigerate a small plate for ½ hour before testing. Take a tablespoon of juice and place on plate. The juice should cool quickly on the refrigerated plate. Check with your finger how thick juice is when cool. If the juice thickens when cool to the consistency of maple syrup, it's ready. If you lift it with a spoon, it should stick to the spoon, not drop like water.
10. Go to **Jam Sealing Instructions** at end of chapter.

Makes two 16-ounce jars

Middle East
Mrabul Teen

Whole Fig Jam

Ingredients
3 pounds fresh green
  figs, preferably harder ones
juice from one lime
4 cups sugar
2 cups water
1.75 ounce box fruit
  pectin (if needed to help thicken)

Preparation

1. ▲**Prepare the figs**: peel the figs' green skin into "zebra stripes," trying not to cut out the white part of the fruit.

2. ▲Heat the water, sugar and lime juice in a large, wide pot on high heat. Bring to a boil and let boil for five minutes. Add the figs, one at a time so they sit on one level.
3. Let cook, uncovered, on very low heat, simmering gently, for two hours. Stir every 15 minutes.
4. After two hours, spoon jam into jars. Go to Step 2 in **Jam Sealing Instructions** at end of chapter.

Makes two 16-ounce jars.

Middle East
Mrabul Freze

Ruby Strawberry Jam

Ingredients
4 pounds strawberries, washed and quartered into pieces
3 1/2 cups sugar
3 tablespoons lemon juice
1.75 ounce box fruit pectin (if needed to help thicken)

Preparation
1. Pour sugar evenly over strawberry pieces in a large bowl. Cover bowl with plastic wrap. Refrigerate overnight, or for at least 12 hours.

2. ▲ In the morning, the fruit will have released a lot of juice into the sugar. There may still be some undissolved sugar in the bottom of the bowl.
3. Pour the fruit, sugar and liquid from the bowl into a pot. Bring to a boil over high heat. Reduce heat to medium and continue boiling, uncovered, stirring occasionally. Boil strawberries for 8 minutes, or until softened.

4. ▲ Remove fruit with a slotted spoon and place cooked fruit into a strainer inside a large bowl.
5. Mix lemon juice into the juices left in the pot. Continue cooking, uncovered, on low-medium heat.

6. ▲ A white foam will develop, especially around the sides of the pot. Spoon off foam and discard. Use a dry spoon to do this.

7. Whatever juice strains from cooked fruit in strainer into bowl, pour back into juice boiling in the pot.
8. Continue boiling juice, uncovered, stirring occasionally, until juice thickens to the consistency of maple syrup.

Note: Test to see if syrup is thick enough: refrigerate a small plate for ½ hour before testing. Take a tablespoon of juice and place on plate. The juice should cool quickly on the refrigerated plate. Check with your finger how thick juice is when cool. If the juice thickens when cool to the consistency of maple syrup, it's ready. Another test is to lift the syrup with a spoon. It should stick to the spoon, not roll off like water.
9. Go to **Jam Sealing Instructions** at end of chapter.

Makes three 16-ounce jars.

Middle East
Mrabul Dirraqin

Surprising Peach Jam

Ingredients
6 pounds peaches, peeled and sliced into thin half-moon slices
6 cups sugar
2 tablespoons lemon juice
1.75 ounce box fruit pectin

Preparation

1. ▲Pour sugar evenly over peach slices in a large bowl. Cover bowl with plastic wrap. Refrigerate overnight, or for at least 12 hours.
2. Pour sugar evenly over peach slices in a large bowl. Cover bowl with plastic wrap. Refrigerate overnight, or for at least 12 hours.
3. In the morning, the fruit will have released a lot of juice into the sugar. There may still be some undissolved sugar in the bottom of the bowl.

4. ▲Pour the fruit, sugar, and liquid from the bowl into a pot. Bring to a boil over high heat.
5. Reduce heat to medium and continue boiling, uncovered, stirring occasionally. Boil peaches for 15 minutes, or until softened.

6. ▲Remove fruit with a slotted spoon and place cooked fruit into a strainer inside a large bowl.
7. Mix lemon juice into the juices left in the pot. Continue cooking, uncovered, on low-medium heat for half an hour.

8. ▲A white foam will develop, especially around the sides of the pot.

9. ▲Spoon off foam and discard. It's very important to use a dry spoon when doing this.
10. Whatever juice strains into the bowl from fruit in the strainer, pour back into juice boiling in the pot.
11. Continue boiling juice, uncovered, stirring occasionally until juice thickens to the consistency of maple syrup.

Note: Test to see if syrup is ready: refrigerate a small plate for ½ hour before testing. Take a tablespoon of juice and place on plate. The juice should cool quickly on the refrigerated plate. Check with your finger how thick juice is when cool. If the juice thickens when cool to the consistency of maple syrup, it's ready. If you lift it with a spoon, it should stick to the spoon, not drop like water.

12. Go to **Jam Sealing Instructions** at end of chapter.
Makes 4 16-ounce jars.

Middle East
Mrabul Sefarjil

Quince Jam

Ingredients
4 pounds fresh quince fruit (available in summer at Middle Eastern stores and health food stores)
4 cups sugar
2 cups water
6 tablespoons lemon juice

Preparation
1. Peel quince. They are a very hard fruit, so use a small, sharp knife to peel.
2. Quarter quince and remove seeds. Add the quince pieces to a food processor. Process all fruit into small pieces.
3. If you don't have a food processor, use a grater. Grate whole, peeled quince, slowly turning it. When you get to the core, stop grating (so you don't grate seeds into jam). Discard the core left at the end.
4. Put quince and sugar into a medium soup pot. Refrigerate overnight.
5. In the morning, bring all contents of bowl to a boil on medium-high heat. Reduce heat to low and continue simmering, uncovered, for 2 hours. Slowly add water, a third of a cup at a time, as the quince mixture becomes dry.

Note: Quince is a relatively dry fruit; so you need to add water to it while cooking.
6. Stir in lemon juice. Cook together for 15 minutes.
7. Go to **Jam Sealing Instructions** at end of chapter.
Makes two 16-ounce jars.

Turkey
Portakal Marmelatı

Orange Marmalade

Ingredients
3 pounds seedless oranges(3 large oranges)
3 cups water
6 cups sugar
4 ½ tablespoons lemon juice
1.75 ounce box fruit pectin
3 16-ounce canning jars

Preparation
1. Scrape off outer part of the orange peel with the fine side of a grater (or a small serrated knife) and discard. Leave bottom layer of peel on the oranges.
   Note: Don't scrape all the way down to white part of the orange; the outer part of the oranges should be light orange.
2. Rinse oranges.

3. ▲ Bring water to a boil in a medium pot on high heat. Place scraped oranges in the water. Return to a boil. Boil oranges for 10 minutes, or until softened.
3. Strain oranges and let cool under cold water. Pour out water used to boil oranges.

4. ▲ Cut oranges into very thin, 1/2 - inch pieces. Throw away orange seeds.

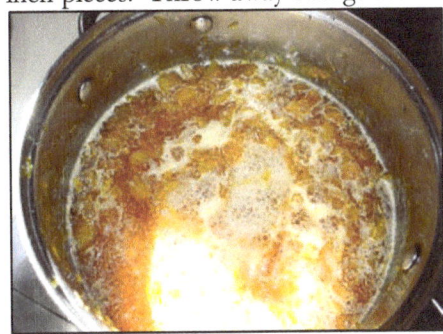

5. ▲ Heat sugar and 3 cups water in a large pot over high heat. Bring to a boil over high heat. Reduce heat to medium-high and continue boiling, stirring occasionally, for 20 minutes, until mixture thickens to the consistency of syrup. Mix in the lemon juice.
6. Mix in cut oranges chunks. Return to a boil, uncovered, on high heat. Reduce heat to medium-high and continue boiling. Boil for 20 minutes, or until soupy.
7. While boiling, combine juice and fruit pectin: Remove ¾ cup of the "juice" the orange chunks are coking in. Mix juice and fruit pectin powder in a small bowl. Set aside.
8. Remove orange pieces from pot with a slotted spoon and place in a bowl. Continue boiling juices for 20 minutes, until thickened.
9. Mix pectin and juice mixture into pot. Turn off the heat.
10. Go to **Jam Sealing Instructions** at end of chapter.

Makes 3 16-ounce jars marmalade.

Middle East Makdous

Walnut-Stuffed Eggplant Pickles

Ingredients
- 10 small eggplants (approximately 3 by 2 inches)
- 2 teaspoons salt
- 40 cloves garlic, finely chopped
- 1 ½ cups chopped walnuts
- 2 tablespoons hot crushed chili pepper (optional)
- 3 cups olive oil

Preparation

place eggplants in a large pot with enough water to cover. Bring to a boil over high heat. Boil for 15 minutes. Remove eggplants with a slotted spoon and place in a bowl of cold water. Gently remove the stems from the eggplant; the stem will come off easily with your fingers, leaving a well rounded end on the eggplant.

Note: If the stem doesn't come off easily, it will need to cook a few more minutes.

deep slit in the side of each eggplant, being careful not to go through the ends or the other side of the eggplant. The slit should only be on one side. Continue with all the eggplants.

1. ▲ **Prepare eggplants for stuffing**:

2. ▲ With a small knife, cut a long and

3. ▲ Rub salt into slit of each eggplant. Place in a plastic strainer. To drain excess liquid, place a small plate over the eggplant and place a jar or a can on top of the plate. Let sit over night in the sink or over a baking sheet (so water doesn't spill everywhere).

4. ▲ **Prepare the stuffing:** mix the garlic, walnuts, and hot chili peppers together. Stuff each eggplant well with the stuffing.

5. Place in a small glass jar. Place each eggplants on its side with the filling side to the outside of the jar.

6. ▲ Once all the eggplants are in the jar then use 2-3 plastic spoons to form an X on the top of the jar. This will hold the eggplants in place.

7. ▲ Turn upside down on a large tray. Let sit like this overnight.

8. Then, the next day, remove spoons and pour olive oil into the glass jar. The olive oil should cover all the eggplant, but leave a ½-inch empty at the top. Keep jars uncovered and on a large tray for at least 3 days.

Note: There will be extra water and gas that is released from the eggplants. This release will bubble the oil out of the jars, so you may need to add more oil to replace what comes out.

9. ▲ Use a butter knife to help release the extra water and gas. To do so, place the butter knife down the side of the jar (be careful not to pierce the eggplant) and apply gentle pressure. You will see air bubbles rise and release.

10. Fill the jars with more oil, if needed, and place the lid on tightly. Leave the eggplants to cure for at least 10 days before opening. This ensures that the eggplants have absorbed the garlic and walnut flavors. *Maqdous* should be stored in a cool, dark place. Serve at room temperature with bread.

Serves 10

Jam Sealing Instructions

1. When juice is thickened, place fruit back into the pot. Be careful not to let the juice burn. If, after half an hour, the jam is still too liquid, mix in a 1.75 ounce box of fruit pectin to help it thicken.

2. Spoon fruit jam into jars while still hot. Fill a 16-ounce jar, leaving a ½-inch empty at the top. Continue until all the jam is used up; it will fill between 2-4 16–ounce jars; depending on the amount of fruit. Seal the jars with their lids.

3. ▲When sealed, place jars in a large pot of boiling water. In the bottom of the pot place an old metal lid or a metal vegetable steamer (old-fashioned metal vegetable steamer that keeps the veggies above the boiling water). Boil for 20 minutes.

4. ▲After boiling, the lids will loosen a bit. Remove from water with tongs and tighten lids. Turn jars upside-down on a tray. This will "vacuum seal" jam, for it to be preserved well.

Note: Test to see if the jars are well sealed by pressing the lid down in the middle. If the lid "moves" or makes a noise, then it's not sealed properly. The lid should be down in a slight U-shape and not move.

5. Let jars cool upside-down. The jam will thicken somewhat as it cools. Ready to serve the next day.

6. Makes 2-4 16-ounce jars, depending on recipe.

Dessert Chapter

Labors of Love

The rose is a special flower which imparts happiness and is used for decoration in celebratory events. Traditionally the beautiful scent of a rose is associated with our Master, the best of Creation, the Prophet Muhammad ﷺ. Hajjah Amina ق used to prepare a rose-shaped dessert called *Gül* to celebrate *Mawlid an-Nabi*, the birth of our blessed Prophet ﷺ.

Gül is a delicious delicacy from the Kazan region of Russia, the birthplace of Hajjah Amina ق. After her family's *hijrah,* emigration, from Russia, Hajjah Amina strived to keep her native traditions alive. Thus, she continued to make Russian Islamic desserts in her new homeland, Damascus and even later after moving to Cyprus.

Preparing *Gül* is a true labor of love. The dough is made, rolled out, and then cut into strips. Each strip is then circled around your fingers, to form the shape of a "rose" *(gül)*. Then it is deep fried. The fried *Gül* are then either dipped in cold sugary syrup or sprinkled with powdered sugar. Hajjah Amina ق would also serve this dish to her family and friends on *Eid al-Adha, Eid al-Fitr,* and at weddings. Not only are the pastries beautiful, but they are a lovely way to remember our beloved Prophet ﷺ.

Kazan, Russia
Gül

Rose Pastries

Ingredients

Syrup
4 cups sugar
2 cups water
3 teaspoons lemon juice

Dough
¼ cup milk
½ tablespoon sugar
¼ teaspoon salt
¼ teaspoon baking powder
3 ¼ cups flour
5 egg whites

Note: ▲ Hajjah Naziha separates the white from yolk by tapping the top and bottom of each egg. Then make a small hole in the top and bottom. Then turn the egg so the hole is toward the bowl. The egg white will pour out.

Preparation

1. **Prepare syrup:** Heat sugar and water in a saucepan over high heat. Bring to a boil. Mix in lemon juice. Pour into a large bowl. Set aside to cool.

Note: It is important for the syrup to cool because when the pastries are cooked, they will be hot and immediately dipped into the syrup. If the syrup is cool and the pastries are hot, the pastries will readily absorb the syrup.

2. In a bowl, combine milk, sugar, salt and baking powder. Mix well.

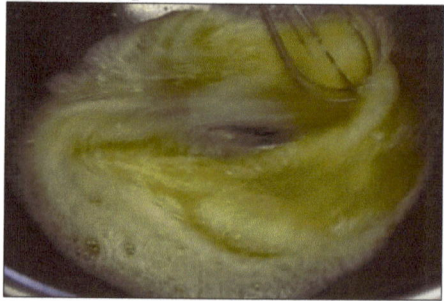

3. ▲ In a separate large bowl, whisk egg whites until bubbly.

4. Whisk milk mixture into egg whites.
5. Slowly stir flour into egg mixture. Knead by hand or use a mixer with a dough hook. Cover dough with two towels and let sit for 15 minutes.

6. ▲ Divide dough into 4 equal parts. Lightly knead each part with your hand. Then let sit, covered by a towel in a warm place for 1 hour (close to a heater or running dryer).

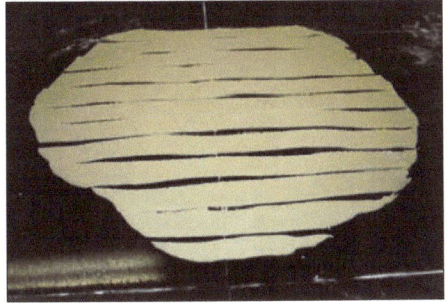

7. ▲ Roll out a dough ball with a rolling pin or *oklava*, a traditional Turkish rolling pin. Roll dough out to 1/16-inch. Then cut out dough into 1-inch strips
8. Form dough into roses: wrap dough around pointer finger and the middle finger, so a long side hangs down.

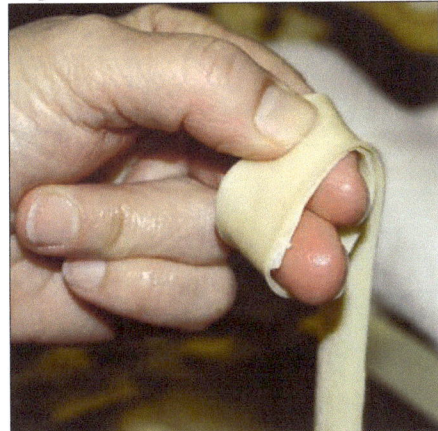

9. ▲ Take the long side of dough and circle around the two fingers.

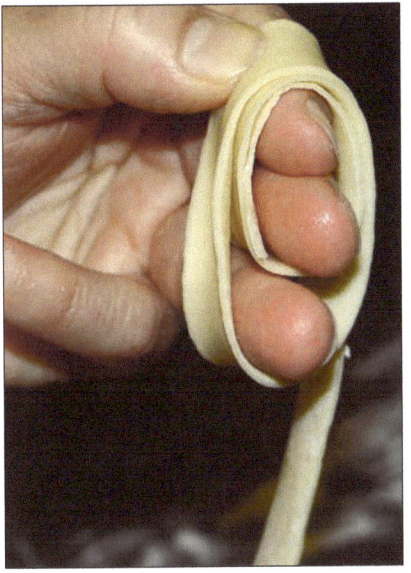

10. ▲ Continue forming the next circle, wrapping the dough around the pointer finger and the ring finger.
11. Continue forming the next circle, circling around the pointer finger and the pinky finger.

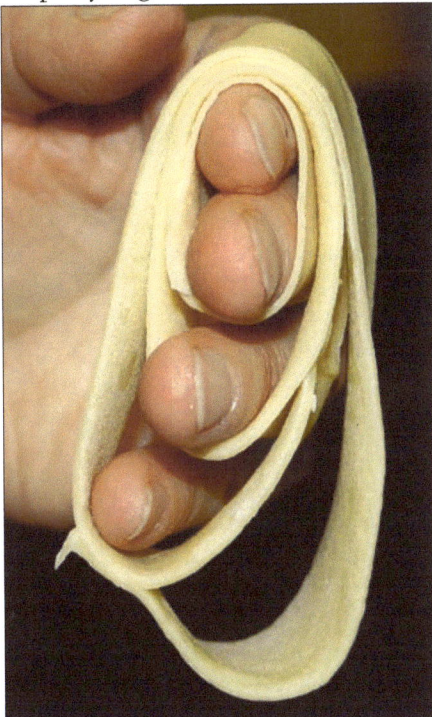

12. ▲ When the dough reaches the end, pinch the end piece very well into the dough underneath it. Make sure it is secure so it won't separate when fried.
13. Continue forming dough roses until all the dough is used up. Keep formed dough roses covered with a towel so it won't dry out.
14. Heat oil for frying on high heat.

15. ▲ Put a fork in center of dough "rose" and immediately place in hot oil. Press lightly down until it becomes golden brown. Turn over and cook other side.

16. ▲ Immediately remove from oil with a slotted spoon (let extra oil drip back into pan). Put into syrup bowl.
17. Coat in syrup. Remove with a slotted spoon (let extra syrup drip back into syrup bowl) and place on serving plate.
18. Repeat Steps 7-16 with remaining dough balls.
Serve immediately.

The above picture shows a serving option good for diabetic people. The pastries are not dipped in syrup, but fried and then sprinkled with a little powdered sugar.

Note: Do not refrigerate. Pastries will keep good for a week. Keep on the counter covered with plastic wrap.

Serves 10-15

Kazan, Russia
Borsok

Golden Fingertip Pastries

Another amazing delicacy from the Kazan region of Russia, the birthplace of Hajjah Amina (q). Similar to the *Gul*, Hajjah Amina (q) would also serve this *Borsok* to her family and friends on *Eid al-Udha*, *Eid al-Fitr*, *Mawlid an-Nabi* and other celebratory days such as weddings.

Borsok are a delicious labor of love. The dough is prepared, then rolled out and cut into strips. The strips are rolled into logs, which are cut into small pieces, deep fried, and then dipped in syrup.

Ingredients
Syrup
- 4 cups sugar
- 2 cups water
- 2 tablespoons lemon juice

Pastries
- 1 cup kefir cultured milk (Usually available in refrigerated section of grocery. If unavailable, use yogurt)
- 4 tablespoons unsalted butter, melted
- ¼ cup warm water
- ½ tablespoon sugar
- ¼ teaspoon salt
- 1¼ teaspoons yeast
- ¼ cup warm milk (heated to 115 degrees)
- 3 ½ cups flour
- 2 cups vegetable oil (for frying)

Preparation

1. **Prepare syrup:** Heat sugar and water in a saucepan over high heat. Bring to a boil. Mix in lemon juice. Let boil together for 5 minutes. Pour into a large bowl. Set aside to cool.

   Note: It is important for the syrup to cool. The pastries, once cooked, must be hot and immediately dipped into the syrup. If the syrup is cool and the pastries are hot, the pastries will readily absorb the syrup.

2. ▲ **Prepare pastries:** Whisk kefir, melted butter, and water in a bowl. Whisk in sugar and salt..

3. In a separate cup, warm water to 115 degrees. Stir in yeast until dissolved. Once yeast has dissolved and mixture is bubbling, whisk sugar and salt into yeast mixture.

4. Slowly whisk in flour. When it gets too thick to stir, add flour and knead by hand for 10 minutes. Knead, until, when you press the dough, it bounces back. The dough will also feel very smooth and should not stick to your fingers.

Note: You can knead by hand or use a mixer with a dough hook.

7. ▲ Take a small piece of dough, the size of a tennis ball. Roll it out with a rolling pin until flat.

10. ▲ Warm oil over high heat. When hot, add small cut pieces of dough and fry until golden brown; they will look like peanuts.

5. ▲ Set dough aside in bowl. Cover with 3 towels. Place dough in a warm place for half an hour, or until dough doubles in size. Then knead again. Cover again with 3 layers of towels and place in a warm place for half an hour, or until dough doubles in size again.

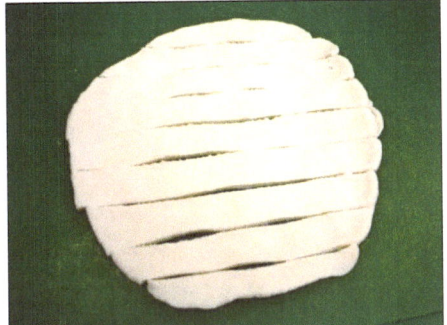

8. ▲ Using a knife, cut dough into ¾-inch wide long strips the entire length of the dough. Continue cutting into strips until all the dough is cut.

11. ▲ Immediately remove from oil with a slotted spoon (let the oil drain off when you lift them) and put directly into the cold syrup bowl.

12. Coat in syrup. Remove with a slotted spoon (let extra syrup drip back into syrup bowl) and place on serving plate.

13. Serve immediately, warm. These are wonderful when served fresh.

14. The leftover pastries will stay good for a week. They should be stored in an airtight container and served at room temperature. Do not refrigerate the leftovers.

Serves 8-10

6. ▲ Remove a piece of dough the size of a tennis ball. Keep extra dough covered at all times. Keep extra balls covered.

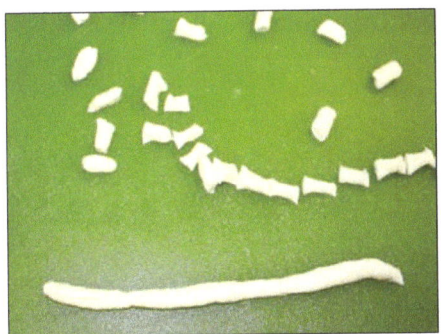

9. ▲ Roll individual dough strips into logs. They will form small logs the thickness of a pen (¼ inch in diameter). Cut round strips into small pieces, about ½-inch-¾-inch long.

Cyprus
Simit Helvası

Almond and Semolina Wheat Sweet

Ingredients
1 cup whole almonds
1 pound (4 sticks) butter
slivered almonds (for garnish)
2 pounds (32 ounces) semolina

Syrup
8 cups water
6 cups sugar

Preparation
1. Put whole almonds into a small pot. Fill with water. Bring to a boil over high heat and continue to boil for two minutes, or until skin pops off easily.
Note: To test, remove an almond from the pot. Rinse under cold water and squeeze. If skin comes off easily, they're done.
2. Remove from heat. Remove skin from all almonds. Cut all almonds in half from the thin side of the almond.
3. **Prepare syrup:** Mix water and sugar in a saucepan. Bring to a boil over high heat. Reduce heat to low and keep warm on the stove.

4. ▲Meanwhile, melt butter in a large pot and add the peeled, cut almonds. Sauté in butter for a minute or two, or until slightly golden.

5. ▲Then stir in the semolina.

6. ▲Cook the semolina, stirring constantly, until the mixture begins to darken somewhat, you get a good toasty smell, and the almonds start to become a golden brown. When the almonds become golden brown, you know the semolina is brown enough.

Note: You have to stir constantly for several minutes. If you leave this, it will burn.

7. ▲Remove from heat and add the hot sugar syrup with a soup ladle. Do this carefully as it will boil and steam a lot. Keep stirring for about 3 minutes to let the semolina absorb the syrup.
8. The semolina mixture will become extremely thick, and harder to stir. Stir until the remaining syrup is well absorbed.
9. To serve, use an ice cream scooper and scoop out the balls of halvah unto a serving plate. Serve in rounds. Garnish with slivered almonds.
10. Serve at room temperature or cold in the summer.
Serves 10-15

Cyprus
Pekmezli Un Helvası

Molasses-Infused Squares

Ingredients
1 cup whole almonds
9 tablespoons butter
6 tablespoons vegetable oil
3 cups white flour

Syrup
2 cups sugar
6 cups water
1 cup grape molasses

Preparation
1. Put almonds into a small pot. Fill with water. Bring to a boil over high heat and boil the almonds for 2 minutes, or until the skin pops off easily.
   Note: To test, remove an almond from the pot. Rinse under cold water and squeeze. If the skin comes off easily, they're done.
2. Remove from heat. Remove skin from all almonds. Cut all almonds in half from the thin side of the almond.

3. ▲ Warm butter and oil over medium heat in a large pot. When the butter is melted, stir in the almonds. Sauté until they start to turn golden.

4. ▲ Then add flour, stirring constantly, so the mixture doesn't burn.

5. In a separate pot, boil sugar and water to make the syrup. When sugar dissolves, add molasses.

6. ▲ Once flour mixture is brownish, ladle the syrup into the flour mixture.

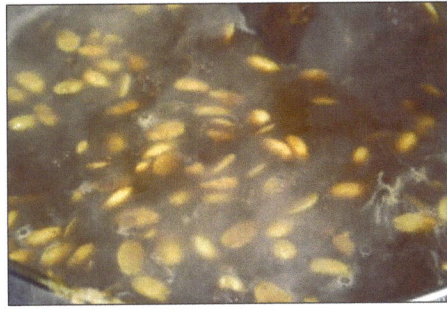

7. ▲ Stir constantly until all the syrup has soaked in. The mixture will get harder to stir as it thickens. It will be thick and solid.

8. ▲ Spread evenly in a serving tray. Let cool and cut into squares.
9. Serve at room temperature.
Serves 6-8

Cyprus
Şekerli Nurlu Börek

Sweet Cheese-Filled Pastry

Ingredients
Dough
2 cups water
½ cup corn oil
½ teaspoon salt
6 ½ cups flour
5 cups vegetable oil (for frying)

Filling
1 gallon whole organic milk
3 ½ tablespoons lemon juice; from fresh lemons
1 ¼ cups sugar + 3 tablespoons sugar
1 teaspoon ground cinnamon

Preparation
1. Make dough. Mix water, oil, and salt. Add flour a little at a time. If dough is too stiff or hard, add water by dampening hands and working into dough. Knead dough by hand, or use a mixer with a dough hook, until it forms a large ball a bit tougher than the consistency of an earlobe. Set aside in a bowl covered with a damp towel.
2. Break dough into thirds. The dough will be rolled out a third at a time. Keep the dough balls covered in a bowl under a towel.

3. ▲ **Prepare cheese filling**: Heat milk in a soup pot on high heat, stirring occasionally. Once it boils, turn off the heat, but keep on the stove. Stir in lemon juice. As soon as you do, the milk will curdle. Let sit for ten minutes.

4. ▲ Pour in a metal sieve put over a bowl. Let strain for 10-15 minutes, and "cheese" will form in the bowl; it should look like a thick cottage cheese.

5. Cover filling and refrigerate for one hour, or until cool.
6. Remove from refrigerator. Break cheese with spoon to break up the big chunks, until fluffy. Set aside.

7. ▲ Mix sugar and cinnamon into cheese. Set aside. Divide filling into thirds in the bowl (so you use a third for each piece of dough).

8. Roll out dough for the pastry to 1/16-inch. Then divide the dough circle in half, marking the halfway line with your rolling pin.

9. ▲ Place the filling on the dough, a heaping half tablespoonful at a time. Flatten filling slightly with hand; and place in straight rows going across and up and down. Fold the empty half of dough over the filled part, creating a half-circle shaped dough with lumps of filling inside.

10. ▲ **Seal the pastries:** First, seal the outer U-shaped edge of dough. Press down with fingertips to seal the dough together.

11. ▲ Then press with your fingertips in vertical lines going down around the bumps of filling. Then press with your fingertips in horizontal lines

12. ▲ Use the edge of a Turkish coffee saucer or a pizza cutter to cut the dough along the pressed lines.

Note: If the pastries open when you are breaking them off, just press the edges of the dough together around the filling to reseal.

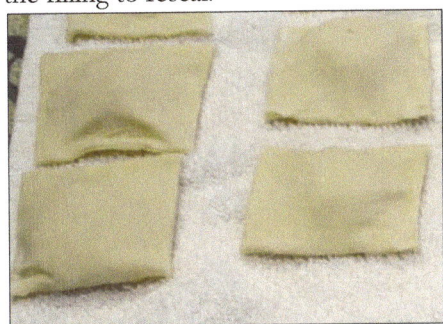

13. ▲ Place filled dough rectangles on a tray covered with a towel. The pastries should be about 2½ inches by 2 inches when filled and before frying.
14. Heat two cups of corn oil on high heat. Test to see if oil is hot enough by dropping in a small piece of dough. If dough bubbles and floats to the top immediately, the oil is ready. If not, wait until it's hot enough

15. ▲ Fry 4 or 5 pastries at a time, until golden on the bottom. Then flip and fry on the other side. They will cook very quickly, so be sure to keep a close eye on them and don't let them burn. Place on a tray.
16. If there are scraps of dough left that don't have any filling, just fry in the oil, remove and sprinkle with sugar; these are also very good.
17. Serve warm or at room temperature on a large platter.

Makes 126 pastries! Each third of dough makes 42.

Middle East
Ashura

Wheat Pudding

A traditional Middle Eastern dish made for Ashura, or the tenth of Muharram. Muharram is the first month of the Islamic lunar calendar. On Ashura throughout history many momentous events have taken place—some tragic and some wondrous. One of these events is that the Ark of Prophet Noah (peace be upon him) finally reached land after sailing for 40 days following the Great Flood. To celebrate, all the remaining dried provisions (various grains, beans, dried fruits, and nuts) were cooked together with sugar to form a sweet dessert. To commemorate the occasion, we make a similar dessert using dried goods. We had the opportunity to be with Hajjah Naziha for this past Ashura. The night before she cooked the wheat and soaked the beans to prepare this special dessert. It is well worth the effort.

Ingredients
½ cup dried apricots
½ cup sliced almonds
¼ cup orange blossom water
¼ cup dry white beans + ¼ tsp baking soda
¼ cup dry black eyed peas + ¼ tsp baking soda
¼ cup dry fava beans + ¼ tsp baking soda
¼ cup dry chick-peas + ¼ tsp baking soda
3 cups sugar
½ cup raisins
1 cup wheat
8 cups water, divided

Garnish
shredded coconut
sliced almonds
chopped pistachios

Preparation
1. If cooking in a pressure cooker, skip to Step 2. If cooking in a pot, put 5 cups water and add wheat. Bring to a boil, covered, on high heat. Reduce heat to medium and partially uncover pot. Boil for 30-40 minutes, or until wheat "opens" (or doubles in size). Turn off heat and remove from stove. Go to Step 3.
2. In a pressure cooker put 4 cups water and add wheat. Place lid on. Bring to a boil on high heat. Once it boils and starts to whistle, reduce heat to low and cook for 10 minutes. Turn off heat and remove from stove.

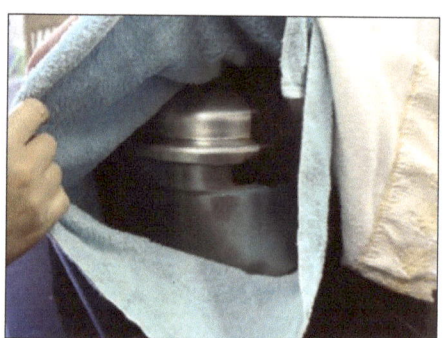

3. ▲Place many large towels over and around the pot (or pressure cooker) to keep it warm. Keep covered with towels overnight.

4. ▲Soak each of the beans in separate bowls with hot water and ¼ teaspoon baking soda. Soak overnight.

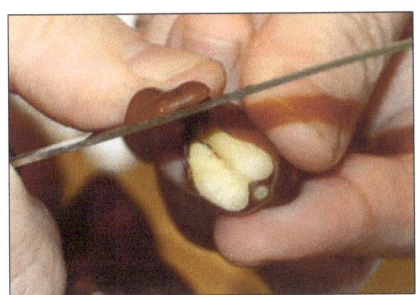

5. ▲In the morning remove the dark skin from the fava beans by cutting them on the side with a small knife.

6. ▲Drain beans. Use fresh water to boil each type of the beans in separate pots. Add 4 cups water to each pot and bring to a boil on high heat. Reduce heat to medium. Continue to boil uncovered, for approximately 10 minutes, or until beans are tender but firm. Drain and rinse.

7. Cut the raisins in half if the raisins are big. Quarter the apricots.

8. Soak raisins in hot water for 5 minutes. Soak apricots separately in hot water for 5 minutes.

9. ▲Add all the beans to wheat pot. Add raisins, apricots, almonds, sugar, and 4 cups water. Bring to a boil, uncovered, on high heat.

10. ▲Reduce heat to medium and simmer, uncovered, for 1 ½ hours, stirring occasionally. Stir in orange blossom water.

Note: The sugar is added at the end of making Ashura because if you add it sooner it will keep the wheat from "opening," from cooking properly.

11. Transfer to serving bowls. Garnish with coconut, almonds, and pistachios.

12. Serve warm or refrigerate and serve cold.

Serves 4-6

Orange-Infused Ashura Wheat Pudding

Hajjah Nazihe's special adaptation of this classic Middle Eastern dish.
Ashura bil burtukal

A non-traditional, but delicious Ashura. Orange juice and orange peel are added to the traditional Ashura for a refreshing change.

Ingredients

The **Orange-Infused Ashura Wheat Pudding** *Ashura bil burtukal* has the same ingredients as the **Wheat Pudding** *Ashura* with 4 changes:
1. Change water amount to 6 cups water.
2. Change sugar amount to 3 1/2 cups powdered sugar
3. Add **1 cup orange juice** to ingredients.
4. Add **½ cup orange peel** cut to 1-cm cubes.

Preparation

Follow Steps 1-8 of the **Wheat Pudding** *Ashura*. Go to Step 9 below:

9. Add all the beans to wheat pot. Add raisins, apricots, almonds, 2 cups water, and sugar.

10. ▲ Add orange juice and orange peel. Boil together for 30 minutes, stirring occasionally.

11. Transfer to serving bowls. Decorate with coconut, almonds, and pistachios.
12. Serve warm or cold.

Serves 4-6

Cyprus
Sütlü Aşure

Milk Wheat Pudding

A creamier version of the traditional Ashura.

Ingredients
The **Milk Wheat Pudding** *Sutlu Ashura* has the same ingredients as the **Wheat Pudding** *Ashura* with 2 changes:
1. Change sugar amount to 2 ¾ cup sugar.
2. Add **4 cups milk** to ingredients.

Preparation
Follow Steps 1-8 of the **Wheat Pudding** *Ashura*. Go to Step 9 below:
9. Add all the beans to wheat pot. Add raisins, apricots, almonds, 4 cups milk, and sugar. Bring to a boil on high heat. Reduce heat to low and cook for 20-30 minutes. Stir constantly so the milk doesn't burn or stick.
10. Transfer to serving bowls. Decorate with coconut, almonds, and pistachios.
11. Serve warm or cold.

Serves 4-6

Pakistan
Souji ka-Halva

Cardamom Flavored Halva with Raisins

Ingredients
2 ¼ cups water
1¼ - 1½ cups sugar (to taste)
1/8 teaspoon saffron (optional)
1 tablespoon vegetable oil
¼ cup raisins
1 stick butter
10 small cardamom pods
1 cup semolina
½ cup slivered almonds

Preparation
1. Prepare sugar syrup. To a saucepan add: water, sugar, and saffron. Bring to a boil on high heat. Stir to dissolve sugar. Once it boils, keep on stove and turn off heat.
2. In a small frying pan, heat the vegetable oil on medium heat. When hot, add raisins and sauté until puffed up. Set aside.
3. Heat butter in a pot on high heat. When hot, add cardamom.

Note: You can either use freshly ground cardamom (grind in a coffee grinder or small food processor) or just crack the whole pods and use.

4. Sauté cardamom in the butter. When seeds or pods turn a light golden brown, add the semolina wheat. Stir constantly until the semolina becomes golden brown.
5. Stir in sugar syrup slowly and carefully, being careful of the steam. Keep stirring. When the mixture starts to thicken add cooked raisins and almonds. Keep stirring until the halva is thick and comes away from the sides of the pan. The semolina mixture will form one big ball.
6. The dish is done when it forms one big ball. Remove from heat.
7. To serve, use an ice cream scooper and scoop out balls of the halvah unto a serving plate. Or pat down in a baking dish and cut into diamond shapes.
8. Serve warm or cold.
Serves 6-8

Turkey
Fırında Sütlaç

Traditional Burnt Rice Pudding

A traditional rice pudding broiled at the end of cooking to give a thin dark brown crust. It can also be made the more conventional way (no broiling), sprinkled with cinnamon on top before serving.

Ingredients
- 1 ½ cups short-grain white rice + 6 cups water
- 12 cups milk (3 liters)
- 5 cups sugar
- ¾ cup cornstarch dissolved in ½ cup water; becomes a paste
- 3 teaspoons vanilla extract
- 2 egg yolks (optional; used for broiling)

Preparation
1. Wash and drain rice. Place in a small pot with 6 cups of water. Bring to a boil on high heat and boil until tender. Drain in a wire strainer.
2. Heat milk in a large pot.

3. ▲ Add sugar. Stir constantly.

4. ▲ Once the milk boils, add the cooked rice. Stir in vanilla. Let boil for 20 minutes on medium heat. Mix in dissolved cornstarch. Let cook for 5 minutes, stirring, until thickened. If broiling in the oven go to Step 6 If not broiling, sprinkle with cinnamon. Refrigerate and serve cold.

5. ▲ To broil take a half cup of the pudding and mix with the egg yolks.

6. ▲ Pour that over the top of the pudding. Broil for 3-5 minutes, or until brown on top.
7. Refrigerate and serve cold.

Serves 10-12

Russia
Sütlü Tukmaç

Old World Sweet Noodle Pudding

His Eminence Mawlana Shaykh Nazim loves this Russian dessert. It is one of his favorites. A sweet, creamy dessert, slightly thinner than a pudding, with skinny noodles.

Ingredients
10 cups water
7 cups milk
3 cups sugar
2-3 teaspoons orange blossom water (optional)
1/3 portion of noodles from **Fettuccine Noodle** recipe in **Bread and Pasta Chapter**

Preparation
1. Bring 10 cups of water to a boil in a small soup pot. Add noodles and boil for 20 minutes, or until the noodles are cooked.
2. Add milk to the pot. Cook on medium-high heat. Continually stir the milk so it won't burn or curdle.
3. When milk boils, add sugar, and reduce heat to medium. Let cook for five minutes, stirring constantly. It will start to thicken. Once thick, turn off heat. Remove from stove, and stir in orange blossom water.
4. Serve warm or cold.

Serves 8-10

Turkey
Kazan Dibi

"Bottom of the Pot" Milk Pudding

Ingredients
¾ cup butter (1 ½ sticks)
1 cup + 3 tablespoons flour
5 cups milk
2 ½ cups powdered sugar
1 teaspoon vanilla
1/8 teaspoon crushed *mastic*, Gum Arabic, (available at Middle Eastern stores.)

Preparation

1. ▲ Melt butter over high heat in a stainless steel pot. Once melted, reduce heat to medium. Add flour and cook, stirring constantly, for five minutes, or until flour becomes golden.

2. ▲ Slowly add milk. Mix well. Stir in powdered sugar. Continue stirring so mixture doesn't burn or stick. Simmer mixture until it thickens.

3. ▲ Remove from heat when consistency of a thick gravy. Mix in vanilla and mastic. Mix for 10-15 minutes with an electric hand mixer; the pudding will become very light and fluffy. Simmer mixture until it thickens.

4. ▲ Pour mixture into a baking dish 13x9x2-inch. Place baking tray on top of stove over 2 burners on high heat. Let cook for ten minutes.
   Note: Do not stir the pudding, as the unique flavor of this dish comes from the browned pudding that will develop on the bottom of the baking dish.

5. Cook until it becomes brown on the bottom; you are going to smell it browning. The pudding will bubble in the middle, and will stick on the bottom of the tray.

6. Remove from heat and let cool for 1 hour at room temperature before putting in refrigerator. Refrigerate for at least five hours, or overnight, before serving.

7. ▲ Take a large serving spoon. Put the spoon in and scratch from browned bottom of the pan. Take a spoonful and flip so that the browned bottom is visible on top of serving dish. Continue, spoonful by spoonful, until all of pudding is on the serving dish with browned side up.

8. Serve cold.

Serves 6-8

International

Crème Caramel (Flan)

Ingredients

Caramel
1 cup white sugar

Custard
1 12-ounce can evaporated milk
1 14-ounce can sweetened condensed milk
¾ cup whole milk
3 large whole eggs
3 egg yokes
2 teaspoons vanilla extract
1 8-ounce can Nestlé's Media Crema (found in Latin foods section of grocery store) or substitute 1 cup sour cream

Tools
- rubber or wooden spatula for stirring
- 9-inch glass pie plate
- 2 quarts boiling water
- 3-4 inch deep roasting pan
- spotholder

Preparation

1. Preheat oven to 350°F. Place water on stove to boil.

2. ▲ To prepare perfect caramel, you must work slowly and attentively. Pour the sugar into a small saucepan with a heavy bottom. Cook over medium-low heat. Do not leave the pan and do not stir. In 4-5 minutes the sugar will begin to dissolve and get clumpy. Stir slowly without stopping as this is the crucial stage.

3. ▲ In 2-3 minutes the sugar will begin to take color. If you are using a dark-coated pan you won't see the color until the caramel is burned, so place a drop on a white surface to determine the color, which should be a golden copper.

4. Immediately pour the caramel into the pie plate, scraping the saucepan thoroughly. Work quickly as the caramel begins to set right away. Using potholders, carefully tilt the pie plate so the caramel coats halfway up the sides.

Note: If the caramel sets before the pie plate is fully coated, hold it an inch above the hot stove burner to reheat slightly.

5. ▲ Set the pie plate in the roasting pan.
6. Combine milks, eggs, yokes, and vanilla in a blender and blend on low speed for 15 seconds. Add Media Créma (or sour cream) and blend for 10 seconds. Let stand for a minute; spoon off and discard any surface foam.

7. ▲ Follow this step for best results. Open the preheated oven and pull out the oven rack. Place the roasting pan on the rack and carefully pour the custard liquid into the pie plate over the caramel. Don't worry if the caramel makes a cracking sound; this is normal. It will fill the pan to the edge.

8. Very carefully, pour enough boiling water in the roasting pan to submerge the pie plate halfway. Move the rack very gently back into the oven. If a few drops of custard spill into the water bath, don't worry.

9. Bake the custard for 1 ½ to 2 hours, or until lightly browned and the top is set.
   Note: Test doneness by lightly shaking the outer baking pan. If the custard jiggles, continue cooking.

10. Turn off the oven and prop the door open two inches and leave the custard in the water bath for an hour, until it comes to room temperature. Refrigerate a minimum of 4 hours or overnight.
11. Here is a foolproof method of "plating" the flan. Carefully run a sharp paring knife around edge of the custard. Select a 12-inch serving plate with a lip as the caramel is now liquid.

12. ▲ Center the serving plate over the pie plate, and grip both firmly with one hand on each side.

13. ▲ Quickly flip the plates, inverting the custard onto the serving plate. Let sit for a minute. The custard should fall away from the pie plate. If it doesn't, heat a clean tea towel with hot water and drape it over the inverted pie plate to warm the caramel slightly and release the custard. Carefully lift the pie plate away and serve your masterpiece!
14. Serve chilled.

Serves 10

Mediterranean
Güneş Keki

Sun Cake

Ingredients
Sweet Dough
½ cup milk
¼ cup sugar
1 teaspoon salt
½ stick butter, cut into 2 pieces
¼ cup warm water (follow instructions)
1 package yeast
1 egg
2 cups flour

Filling
1/8 cup melted butter
¾ cup finely chopped apples
½ cup sugar
¼ cup chopped pecans or walnuts
1 teaspoon cinnamon

Preparation
1. **Prepare dough:** Heat milk until small bubbles form around edge of pot. Stir in sugar, salt, and butter and remove from heat. Allow butter to melt, stirring now and then. Cool to lukewarm.
2. Put warm water in a large warm bowl (rinse bowl with hot water and dry before using). Sprinkle yeast into water.
3. Stir milk mixture, egg, and half of flour into water and yeast. Beat until smooth. Stir in remaining flour to make a stiff dough. Cover tightly with aluminum foil. Refrigerate for two hours.
4. Preheat oven to 350°F.

5. ▲ Roll out dough until it is a 12 by 17 inch oblong piece. Brush with melted butter.

6. ▲ In a bowl, combine chopped apples, sugar, pecans, and cinnamon. Sprinkle over dough.

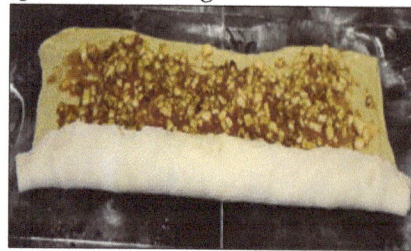

7. ▲ Roll up from long side and seal edges. Place sealed edges down and form a circle.

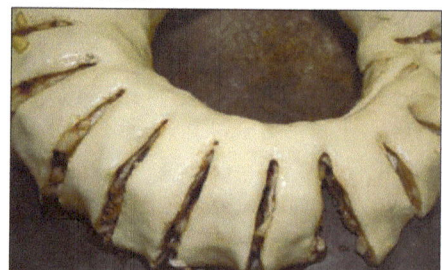

8. ▲ Make ½-inch cuts ¾-inch apart all the way around the outside of ring so that some of the filling shows in small "stripes."

9. ▲ Turn slices to side. Bake on a cookie sheet for 40-50 minutes, or until golden brown.
10. Serve warm.

Serves 4-6

Turkey
Portakal Sütlacı

Zesty Cream-Topped Orange Pudding in Oranges

Ingredients
4 medium-sized oranges
4 tablespoons short-grain rice
1 cup water + 1 cup orange juice (squeezed from oranges)
1 egg yolk
1 box (4.6-ounces or 130 grams) vanilla instant pudding
2 cups milk
whipped cream (for topping)

Topping
½ cup heavy whipping cream
3 teaspoons sugar
¼ teaspoon orange blossom water
½ teaspoon orange zest (optional)

Preparation
1. Rinse off oranges.
2. Core oranges:

a. ▲Cut off tops of oranges. Using a steak knife; cut out inside of oranges. Be careful not to break orange peel. Scoop out orange pulp into a bowl as you core.

b. ▲Then, using a spoon, remove rest of orange pulp into bowl. Start scraping in one place until you reach the white part of the orange. Then move to the next part of the orange; scraping it again from the white part. Again, be careful not to tear the peel. Scrape completely, until the orange peel is like an empty cup. There may be a little orange pulp left in the very bottom, where the blossom is; just leave it so peel is not damaged.
3. Place orange pulp in a metal strainer over a bowl to get fresh orange juice. You may need to mash the pulp a little to get enough juice out, depending on how juice the oranges are. You need one full cup of orange juice.
4. Boil rice in 1 cup of water. Bring to a boil on high heat; then reduce heat to medium and cook, covered, until rice is soft. Stir occasionally.
5. Stir orange juice into the softened rice. Bring to a boil on high heat. Reduce heat to medium and continue cooking, uncovered, until the rice absorbs the juice.
6. Beat the egg yolk in a small bowl. Stir into pot of rice and orange juice. Turn off heat and let cool.
7. In a separate bowl, whisk instant pudding and milk. Add rice mixture to pudding. Mix well.

8. ▲Spoon rice pudding mixture into oranges. Fill oranges about three quarters of the way full, leaving a half inch empty at the top (for topping).
9. Chill in refrigerator for at least an hour.
10. Blend whipping cream with a mixer until it forms firm peaks.
   Note: If using prepared whipping cream, put on just before serving as it becomes flat quickly.
11. Slowly add sugar and orange blossom water to whipped cream. Fold in orange zest.
12. Put mixture in a pastry bag. (You can also use a Ziploc bag by filling with the topping, cutting off the corner, and squeezing from cut corner.)
13. Pipe topping on top of oranges.
14. Sprinkle with a little orange zest for decoration.
15. Refrigerate and serve cold.
Serves 4.

America

Chilled Berry Meringue

Ingredients

2 cups fresh berries(strawberries, blueberries, or raspberries)
3 egg whites
½ cup + 3 tablespoons sugar, divided

Preparation

1. Wash berries of your choice under cold water. If using strawberries remove stem.

2. Mash berries with the bottom of a glass or blend in blender. Set aside 1 cup of the crushed berries to mix into the meringue. Cover and refrigerate.

3. Sweeten remaining 1 cup of crushed berries with ½ cup of the sugar. Cover and refrigerate until ready to serve.

4. **Form the meringue:** In a large bowl beat egg whites on medium-high until they form firm white peaks. Add remaining 3 tablespoons of sugar, a tablespoon at a time.

5. ▲ Add unsweetened cup of crushed berries to meringue mix.

6. ▲ Mix well.

7. Place in a covered plastic container in the freezer for 1 hour, or until solid.

8. To serve, spoon sweetened, refrigerated crushed berries into serving bowls. Then, using an ice cream scoop, top with frozen berry meringue.

9. Serve cold.

Serves 4

Turkey
Şeftali Muhallebisi

Light Peach Pudding

A delicious, flavorful treat guaranteed to please. Very tasty when peaches are ripe and sweet, at the peak of their season in summer.

Ingredients
4-5 fresh ripe peaches
3-5 tablespoons sugar

Note: If peaches are more ripe and sweet, 3 tablespoons sugar is enough. If not ripe, more sugar is needed.

1 cup water
1 ½ tablespoons cornstarch dissolved in 3 tablespoons cold water

Preparation
1. Cut 4 slices of peach (with peel) to decorate serving cups. Set aside.
2. If peaches are hard, place peaches in bowl of hot water to peel easily. Let sit for 5 minutes. If peaches are very soft, there is no need to soak peaches and the dish will be more delicious and juicy.
3. Peel peaches and remove pits. Peel carefully so not too much fruit is removed. Cut peaches into pieces. Discard peel and pits.
4. Blend peach pieces in blender until very smooth and juicy. Pour from blender into metal strainer over a bowl. Push down on strainer with back of spoon to press peach puree into bowl. Pour peach puree into cup measure; there should be about 1 cup of peach puree.
5. **In a small saucepot add:** puree and sugar. Bring to a boil on medium-high heat. Mix in dissolved cornstarch.
6. Mix puree and cornstarch briefly over heat. Remove from heat. Pour into serving cups. Decorate with reserved peach slices. Refrigerate until cold.
7. Serve cold.

Serves 4

Bosnia
Tufahije

Pureed Walnut Stuffed Apples

Ingredients
9 apples
2 cups sugar
3 cups water
1 ¼ cups walnuts
Topping
¼ cup whipping cream
1 ½ tablespoons sugar
sprinkle with grated chocolate

Preparation

1. ▲Core and peel apples. Use an apple corer to remove apples' centers. A hole should go completely through the apples. Place apples in a bowl of water so they don't brown.
2. **Prepare syrup:** Mix sugar and water in a pot. Bring to boil over high heat.

3. ▲Place cored apples in boiling syrup. When apples are in syrup, they will float to top. Continuously press them back into the syrup, and make sure syrup goes into the hole in center of apple. Cook for 5-10 minutes, or until softened but still firm.

Note: Cooking time will vary based on apple size and type. Some apples will soften in just 5 minutes. Don't let them get too soft or they will crumble when stuffed.
4. Remove apples from syrup and let cool for 30 minutes.

5. ▲Process walnuts to the size of wheat grains. They will resemble bulgur after processing in a food processor.
In a bowl, combine half a cup of sugar syrup with ground walnuts. Mix well. The syrup sweetens and softens the walnuts. The mixture should resemble a thick paste.

6. ▲Place apples on a serving dish. Fill apples with walnut mixture, using a teaspoon and your fingers. Put some of the syrup in the serving dish around the apples.
7. In a separate bowl, beat the whipping cream until firm peaks form. Slowly add the sugar.
8. Place a spoonful of whipped cream on the top of the apples and sprinkle with the grated chocolate. Refrigerate for 2-4 hours, or until cold.
9. Serve cold.

Serves 9.

Turkey
Çikolatalı Armut Tatlısı

Walnut and Raisin Stuffed Pears

Ingredients
5 pears
½ cup golden raisins
1 cup walnuts, finely chopped
1 cup powdered sugar
¾ cup water
½ cup milk chocolate chips
2 tablespoons pistachios, finely chopped

Preparation
1. Preheat oven to 300°F.

2. ▲ Peel and core pears. If possible, use an Arab corer (a long thin instrument).
3. Put raisins in a bowl of hot water. Let soak for a couple minutes to soften. Drain. Mix raisins and walnuts in a medium bowl.

4. ▲ Stuff cored pears with walnut and raisin mixture. Place in 8-inch by 8-inch baking dish.

5. ▲ Mix sugar and water. Pour into bottom of the baking dish, and over the pears. Bake uncovered for 2 hours and 15 minutes, or until soft. Every half hour, open oven and spoon sugar syrup (from bottom of pan) over top of pears.
6. Melt chocolate chips in a double boiler. Put chips in a metal bowl on top of a small pot of boiling water. When chocolate is melted, evenly pour over top of each pear.
7. To garnish, sprinkle the top of each pear with pistachios.
8. Serve warm or at room temperature.

Serves 5

Lebanon
Gatto bit Tamar wal Joz

Spiced Date Bread with Walnuts

Ingredients
1 cup dates (approximately 15 dates), pitted and chopped
1 cup raisins
1 cup boiling water
1 egg
1 cup sugar, sifted
3 tablespoons butter, softened
1½ cups flour
¼ teaspoon salt
1 ½ teaspoons baking powder
¼ teaspoon baking soda
1 teaspoon cinnamon
1 cup walnuts, finely chopped

Preparation
1. Preheat oven to 350°F.
2. Place dates and raisins in bowl. Cover with boiling water. Let soak for 5 minutes.
3. In a small bowl, beat the egg.
4. Mix sugar, butter and egg until smooth, preferably with a mixer.
5. **In a separate bowl combine dry ingredients:** flour, salt, baking powder, baking soda, and cinnamon. Mix well.
6. Then slowly add dry ingredients to wet ingredients, a third at a time. Mix in the dates, raisins, and their water.
7. Mix in walnuts.
8. Grease and flour bread pan. Pour in batter. Even out top.
9. Bake for 45 minutes, or until a fork inserted in bread comes out clean.

Serves 4-6

Turkey
Portakallı Pirinç Helvası

Orangey Rice and Coconut Bars

Ingredients
2 cups short grained white rice
2 cups hot water (for soaking rice)
4 cups milk
4 cups water for cooking
1 cup shredded coconut
2 cups powdered sugar, divided
Note: If you don't have powdered sugar, use regular sugar and blend it in a blender. It becomes powdered sugar.
2 ¼ cups slivered almonds, divided
3 eggs
3 tablespoons butter
zest (grated peel) from one orange
1 teaspoon vanilla essence
1 cup of orange juice
butter (to grease pan)

Preparation
1. Preheat oven to 350°F.
2. Soak rice in 2 cups hot water for at least 10 minutes. Drain rice.
3. Heat milk and water in a pot on high heat. Once it boils, add drained rice to milk. Reduce heat to medium. Cook rice and milk together, stirring occasionally, untill rice is tender.

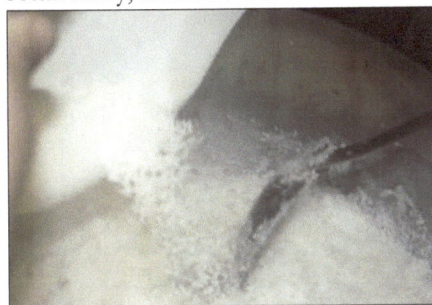

4. ▲ Add one cup of sugar and coconut to the milk and rice. Reduce heat to low. Cover and cook for 35 minutes.

5. ▲ Melt butter in a saucepan. When slightly cooled, whisk in the eggs. Mix in the orange zest and cup almonds .
6. Grease a 9x13 Pyrex baking dish with butter. Spread ¾ cup almonds on the bottom of the baking dish.

7. ▲ Mix half of the butter and egg mixture into the milk and rice mixture. Pour into the Pyrex dish. Even out top with a spoon; press slightly to compact.

8. ▲Spread remaining half of the butter and egg mixture evenly on top, a little at a time.
9. Bake for 20 minutes. Then broil the rice bars for 5-10 minutes, or until golden brown.
10. **While baking, prepare syrup:** Mix the vanilla, orange juice, and the sugar (1 cup) in a small pot. Boil together for 3 minutes.

11. ▲ Pour the syrup on top of the rice bars. Use a toothpick to poke holes into the rice bars. These holes will allow the syrup to be absorbed into the rice bars.
12. Sprinkle ¾ cup of almonds on top. Let cool. Then cut into bars.
13. Serve at room temperature.
Serves 6-8.

Turkey
Havuç Peltisi

Zesty Orange and Carrot Aspic

Ingredients
4 carrots, peeled
1 ½ cups powdered sugar
6 tablespoons corn starch
3 cups water
2 cups orange juice
1 Tablespoon vanilla
Whipped cream (optional) for garnish

Preparation
1. Cut carrots into large pieces. Grate carrots in food processor with largest grating disc (or grate with grater).

2. ▲ **In a saucepan add:** carrots and powdered sugar. Cook on low heat. Cook for approximately 10 minutes, or until carrots are soft.

3. **In a separate small saucepan add:** water and cornstarch. Bring to a boil on high heat, stirring constantly. Once it starts to thicken, add orange juice and vanilla. Mix well. Boil together for 10 minutes, or until it starts to thicken. It should look like pudding.

4. ▲ Pour into a mold (a pie pan or decorative cake mold.)
5. Place filled mold inside a larger pan filled with icy cold water. Put both pans in refrigerator to cool. Leave overnight.
6. In the morning, to remove aspic from the mold, place mold in pan of larger pan filled with hot water. Let sit for one minute. Put a plate over the mold and flip over the plate.
7. Garnish with whipped cream.
8. Serve cold.

Serves 4-6

Lebanon
Al-Maziah

Zesty Grapefruit Pudding

Ingredients
1 large grapefruit
3 cups milk
1 cup water
2 ½ cups powdered sugar
3 tablespoons corn starch
5 tablespoons flour
½ cup water

Preparation
1. Peel grapefruit. Remove skin from the grapefruit slices. Cut into small ¼-inch pieces. Reserve a few grapefruit pieces for garnish in a small bowl.
2. **In a small saucepan add:** milk, water, and powdered sugar. Bring to a boil on high heat, stirring constantly.
3. **In a small bowl add:** cornstarch, flour, and water. Mix well. Add to milk mixture, stirring constantly. It will start to thicken. Boil for 2-3 minutes, or until it thickens to the consistency of pudding. Remove from heat.
4. Add grapefruit slices and mix well. Place in a serving dishes or cups. Top with reserved grapefruit slices. Place in refrigerator.
5. Serve cold.

Serves 3-4

Lebanon
Cake bil Jibne Crema

Creamy Grapefruit Crumble

Ingredients
2 cups graham cracker crumbs
2 teaspoons lemon zest
6 tablespoons butter, melted
2 grapefruits
3 oranges
2 egg whites
1/3 cup sugar + 3 tablespoons sugar
1 whole egg
16 ounces cream cheese
2 ½ tablespoons Orange Jello
3 tablespoons orange juice + 1 tablespoon orange juice
1 ½ tablespoons lemon juice
2 tablespoons orange zest
1 cup shredded coconut
1 cardboard circle cakeboard (often used for bakery cakes) to use as a liner, available at craft stores

Preparation
1. Put cakeboard in spring-form pan.
2. **Prepare crust:** in a small bowl combine graham cracker crumbs, lemon zest, and melted butter. Mix well. Press into cakeboard liner in spring-form pan. Press crumbs flat to form a crust onbottom.

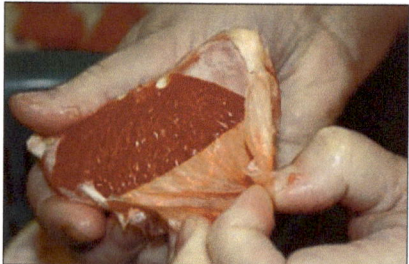

3. ▲Prepare all the zests before starting and squeeze juices. Measure and set aside. Peel and take the skin from the slices of grapefruit and oranges. Cut grapefruits and oranges into small pieces.

4. Place egg whites in a large bowl. Beat egg whites with a mixer until they form white peaks, then slowly add the 3 tablespoons sugar. Beat well.
5. Bring water in the bottom of a double boiler to a boil on high heat.
6. Meanwhile, in a small bowl, mix the whole egg and 1 tablespoon of the orange juice. Mix well.

7. Pour the egg and orange juice into the top of the double boiler. Stir constantly. Once it starts to thicken, remove quickly from the heat and continue to stir. Add cooked egg to the whipped egg whites.
8. **In a separate bowl add:** cream cheese, Jello, sugar, orange juice, lemon juice, and orange zest. Mix well. Add egg white mixture. Mix well.

9. ▲Add oranges and grapefruit that are cut into small pieces. Mix with the cream cheese mixture. Pour over the crust. Sprinkle with coconut over the top and chill for 10-12 hours or overnight.
10. Serve cold.
Serves 6-8

Turkey
Melek Öpücüğü

Angel Kisses

Ingredients
Meringues
4 egg whites
1 cup powdered sugar
1 teaspoon cinnamon
Filling
1 ounce chocolate (dark, milk, or white)
2 ½ tablespoons

Preparation
1. Preheat oven to 225°F degrees
2. Line 2 cookie sheets with wax paper.
3. **Prepare meringues:** using an electric mixer on high speed, beat egg whites.
4. When egg whites start to form peaks, slowly add sugar and cinnamon until all sugar and cinnamon is added.

5. ▲ Continue beating egg whites until they hold stiff peaks.

6. ▲ Put the meringue into a pastry bag.

7. ▲ Then pipe the meringue onto the cookie sheets, forming pyramid-like "kisses," using the large star head on the pastry bag. The meringues should have a 2-inch diameter at the base.
5. Bake for one and a half hours. Turn off oven but leave meringues inside oven to cool (as the oven cools) for one hour. This method of cooling ensures the meringues stay crispy.

8. ▲ Remove cooled meringues from oven. Gently lift meringues off of wax paper.
9. **Prepare filling:** in a double boiler add chocolate and cream. Stir. When melted, remove from heat and stir with a spoon.
10. Using a spatula, spread some chocolate filling unto the wide base of a meringues. Press another meringue on gently to make a "meringue sandwich" with a chocolate center. Continue until all meringues are filled.
11. Serve at room temperature. Store in an airtight container.
Makes 22-32 meringues/16 meringue "sandwiches" with filling.

Index of Recipes

Soup Chapter

Introductory Vignette: Soup through the Ages 1
    1. Smooth Red Lentil and Carrot Soup 2
    2. Yogurt and Rice Soup 3
    3. Creamy Chicken Soup 4
    4. Beef Chunk and Rice Soup 5
    5. Fettuccine and Lentil Soup 6
    6. Pomegranate-Flavored Fettuccine and Lentil Soup 7
    7. Creamy Tomato Soup 8
    8. Carrot Soup 9
    9. Leek Soup 10

Salad Chapter

Introductory Vignette: Eyes Eat Before the Mouth..11
    1. Green Fava Bean Preparation 12
    2. Fresh Fava Beans and Garlic 13
    3. Green Olive and Cilantro Salad 14
    4. Beet Salad 15
    5. Cabbage Salad 16
    6. Carrot and Radish Salad 17
    7. Eggplant Salad 18
    8. Fava Bean Salad 19
    9. Parsley-Flavored Potato and Egg Salad 20
    10. Roasted Bell Pepper Salad 21
    11. Tomato and Cucumber Salad 22
    10. Zucchini Salad 23

Vegetable Sides Chapter

Introductory Vignette: Mediterranean Vegetable Dishes 25
    1. Cilantro and Garlic-Flavored Potatoes 26
    2. Cumin-Spiced Potatoes 27
    3. Zucchini with Onions and Tomatoes 28
    4. Tangy Cauliflower Florets 29
    5. Chard Stems with Yogurt 30
    6. Dandelion Greens 31
    7. Vegetarian Grape Leaves 32
    8. Vegetarian Stuffed Bell Peppers 34
    9. Chard and Black-Eyed Peas 35
    10. Sauteed Fava Beans with Cilantro and Garlic 36

Egg Chapter

Introductory Vignette: Ahmed and the Disappearing Eggs 37
    1. Eggs and Dates 38
    2. Asparagus Tips and Eggs 39
    3. Fried Eggs with Black Olives 40
    4. Bird's Nest Eggs 41
    5. Golden Fried Cheese with Eggs 42
    6. Sautéed Onions and Mushrooms with Eggs 43
    7. Eggs on a Bed of Sautéed Onions and Spinach 44
    8. Eggs over Garden of Sautéed Vegetables 45

9. Eggs over Savory Cured Meat	46
10. Eggs over Seasoned Ground Beef	47
11. Poached Eggs	48
12. Eggs Scrambled with Golden Potato Cubes	49
13. Onions and Tomatoes Scrambled with Eggs	50
14. Small Sausages and Eggs	51
15. Eggs Scrambled with Spicy Sausage Rounds	52

Bean and Legume Chapter

Introductory Vignette: Openings	53
1. Garbanzo Bean Preparation	54
2. Garbanzo Bean and Parsley Salad	55
3. Buttery Pine Nuts and Garbanzo Beans	56
4. Garbanzo Beans in Yogurt and Tahini	57
5. Crispy Bread Smothered with Garbanzo Beans and Tahini	58
6. Garbanzo Beans and Tahini with Ground Beef Topping	59
7. Fava and Garbanzo Bean Spread	60
8. Spicy Vegetarian Lentil Patties	62

Bread and Pasta Chapter

Introductory Vignette: Significance of Wheat Grains and Bread	63
1. Savory Black Olive Bread and Halloum Cheese Bread	64
2. Fettuccine Noodles	66
3. Bosnian Burek	68
4. Savory Russian Meat Pastries	70
5. Lentil Lasagna	73
6. Cheese-Filled Ravioli	74
7. Ground Beef Filled Dumplings in Broth	76
8. Vignette: Hajjah A'isha's Peel Meen	79
9. Small Meat-Filled Dumplings in Savory Tomato Broth	80

Rice and Bulgur Chapter

Introductory Vignette: Benefits of Rice	83
1. Rice with Fried Noodles	84
2. Jeweled Rice	85
3. Layered Meat, Rice, and Vegetables on a Platter	86
4. Tomato Rice	88
5. Bulgur and Onions	89
6. Green Fava Bean Pilau with Beef Chunks	90

Poultry Chapter

Introductory Vignette: Cypriot Chickens	91
1. Chicken with Bell Peppers	92
2. Chicken and Cauliflower with Béchemal Sauce	93
3. Stuffed Chicken Breasts	94
4. Chicken with Carrots in White Sauce	96
5. Roasted Chicken	97
6. Chicken with Mushrooms and Tomatoes	98
7. Crispy Chicken Over Cheesy Tubular Pasta	99
8. Stuffed Chicken with Savory Rice and Ground Beef	100
9. Meat and Nut-Filled Rice to Accompany Stuffed Chicken	101

Fish Chapter

Introductory Vignette: Importance of Fish 103
    1. Fish Preparation Instructions 104
    2. Fisherman's Rice 105
    3. Baked Salmon with Garlic 106
    4. Spicy Fried Fish 107
    5. Baked Snapper 108
    6. Sultan Ibraheem Fish 109
    7. Grilled Shrimp 110
    8. Coconut Shrimp 111
    9. Curried Shrimp in a Sauce 112
    10. Curried Coconut Shrimp 113
    11. Fish Sauces: Garlic and Lemon Dipping Sauce and Tahini Dipping Sauce 114

Stuffed Vegetable Chapter

Introductory Vignette: Hajjah Naziha and the Stuffed Cucumber 115
    1. Whole Cauliflower Stuffed with Ground Beef 116
    2. Stuffed Onions 117
    3. Artichokes Stuffed with Seasoned Ground Beef 118
    4. Stuffed Zucchini in Yogurt Sauce 120
    5. Stuffed Grape Leaves, Eggplant, and Zucchini 122
    6. Cabbage Leaves Stuffed with Savory Rice and Ground Beef 124
    7. Stuffed Swiss Chard 126
    8. Ground Beef Stuffed Golden Potatoes 128

Beef and Lamb Chapter

Introductory Vignette: Kawarma 129
    Kibbeh Introduction 130
    1. Baked Kibbeh 131
    2. Fried Kibbeh 132
    3. Filled Kibbeh in Seasoned Yogurt Sauce 134
    4. Spicy Raw Ground Beef and Bulgur Mixture 135
    5. Kofta 136
    6. Fresh Fava Beans and Meat Chunks 137
    7. Cilantro-Flavored Beef Pieces and Potatoes 138
    8. Meat with White Beans 139
    9. Stuffed Biftek 140
    10. Meatballs over Bread with Yogurt 142
    11. Musakka 144
    12. Potato and Kafta Patties 146
    13. Potato and Ground Beef Casserole 147
    14. Okra with Meat 148
    15. Thin Steaks with French-Fried Potatoes 150

Juice and Beverages

Introductory Vignette: The Importance of Tea 151
    1. Black Tea 153
    2. Turkish Coffee 154
    3. SK's Iced Mocha: Regular and Decaffeinated Versions 155
    4. Refreshing Yogurt Drink 156
    5. Homemade Orange Juice 157
    7. Pineapple Banana Smoothie 158
    8. Ginger Mango Smoothie 159
    9. Strawberry Milkshake 160

Jam and Preserve Chapter

Introductory Vignette: Traditional Cypriot Jam Making 161
   1. Golden Apricot Jam 162
   2. Cherry Jam 163
   3. Apple Jam 164
   4. Whole Fig Jam 165
   5. Ruby Strawberry Jam 166
   6. Surprising Peach Jam 167
   7. Quince Jam 168
   8. Orange Marmalade 169
   9. Walnut-Stuffed Eggplant Pickle 170
   10. Jam Sealing Instructions 172

Dessert Chapter

Introductory Vignette: Labors of Love 173
   1. Rose Pastries 174
   2. Golden Fingertip Pastries 176
   3. Almond and Semolina Wheat Sweet 178
   4. Molasses-Infused Squares 179
   5. Sweet Cheese Filled Pastry 180
   6. Wheat Pudding 182
   7. Orange-Infused Ashura Wheat Pudding 184
   8. Milk Wheat Pudding 185
   9. Cardamom Flavored Halva with Raisins 186
   10. Traditional Burnt Rice Pudding 187
   11. Old World Sweet Noodle Pudding 188
   12. "Bottom of the Pot" Milk Pudding 189
   13. Crème Caramel (Flan) 190
   14. Sun Cake 192
   15. Zesty Cream-Topped Orange Pudding in Oranges 193
   16. Chilled Berry Meringue 194
   17. Light Peach Pudding 195
   18. Pureed Walnut Stuffed Apples 196
   19. Walnut and Raisin Stuffed Pears 197
   20. Spiced Date Bread with Walnuts 198
   21. Orangey Rice and Coconut Bars 199
   22. Zesty Orange and Carrot Aspic 200
   23. Zesty Grapefruit Pudding 201
   24. Creamy Grapefruit Crumble 202
   25. Angel Kisses 203